CAMBRIDGE LIBRARY COLLECTION

Books of enduring scholarly value

Travel and Exploration

The history of travel writing dates back to the Bible, Caesar, the Vikings and the Crusaders, and its many themes include war, trade, science and recreation. Explorers from Columbus to Cook charted lands not previously visited by Western travellers, and were followed by merchants, missionaries, and colonists, who wrote accounts of their experiences. The development of steam power in the nineteenth century provided opportunities for increasing numbers of 'ordinary' people to travel further, more economically, and more safely, and resulted in great enthusiasm for travel writing among the reading public. Works included in this series range from first-hand descriptions of previously unrecorded places, to literary accounts of the strange habits of foreigners, to examples of the burgeoning numbers of guidebooks produced to satisfy the needs of a new kind of traveller - the tourist.

A Winter in North China

In the winter of 1890, the Reverend T.M. Morris and the Reverend Richard Glover spent five months journeying through the Shantung and Shansi provinces in north China. Commissioned by the Baptist Missionary Society to inspect the work of all missionaries in the area, the two clergymen travelled by boat, cart, wheelbarrow and 'other strange conveyances' in order to complete their mission. Published in 1892, this book compiles the letters sent home by Morris, originally appearing in *The East Anglian Daily Times* and the *Freeman*. Writing with notable Christian zeal, Morris ably describes the difficulties faced in such a journey, delighting at the people encountered and wondering at the awe-inspiring landscape. With a preface by Glover attesting to Morris's 'careful and shrewd' observational skills, and a map of the area covered in this remarkable journey, this book provides a novel insight into nineteenth-century China.

T0370876

Cambridge University Press has long been a pioneer in the reissuing of out-of-print titles from its own backlist, producing digital reprints of books that are still sought after by scholars and students but could not be reprinted economically using traditional technology. The Cambridge Library Collection extends this activity to a wider range of books which are still of importance to researchers and professionals, either for the source material they contain, or as landmarks in the history of their academic discipline.

Drawing from the world-renowned collections in the Cambridge University Library, and guided by the advice of experts in each subject area, Cambridge University Press is using state-of-the-art scanning machines in its own Printing House to capture the content of each book selected for inclusion. The files are processed to give a consistently clear, crisp image, and the books finished to the high quality standard for which the Press is recognised around the world. The latest print-on-demand technology ensures that the books will remain available indefinitely, and that orders for single or multiple copies can quickly be supplied.

The Cambridge Library Collection will bring back to life books of enduring scholarly value (including out-of-copyright works originally issued by other publishers) across a wide range of disciplines in the humanities and social sciences and in science and technology.

A Winter
in North China

T.M. MORRIS
RICHARD GLOVER

CAMBRIDGE
UNIVERSITY PRESS

CAMBRIDGE UNIVERSITY PRESS

Cambridge, New York, Melbourne, Madrid, Cape Town, Singapore,
São Paolo, Delhi, Dubai, Tokyo

Published in the United States of America by Cambridge University Press, New York

www.cambridge.org
Information on this title: www.cambridge.org/9781108013826

© in this compilation Cambridge University Press 2010

This edition first published 1892
This digitally printed version 2010

ISBN 978-1-108-01382-6 Paperback

This book reproduces the text of the original edition. The content and language reflect
the beliefs, practices and terminology of their time, and have not been updated.

Cambridge University Press wishes to make clear that the book, unless originally published
by Cambridge, is not being republished by, in association or collaboration with, or
with the endorsement or approval of, the original publisher or its successors in title.

A WINTER IN NORTH CHINA

A

A

WINTER IN NORTH CHINA

BY THE

REV. T. M. MORRIS

OF IPSWICH

AUTHOR OF 'SERMONS FOR ALL CLASSES,' 'THE MYSTERY OF
THE BURNING BUSH,' ETC., ETC.

WITH AN INTRODUCTION

BY THE

REV. RICHARD GLOVER, D.D.

OF BRISTOL

WITH A MAP

LONDON:
THE RELIGIOUS TRACT SOCIETY
56 PATERNOSTER ROW, 65 ST. PAUL'S CHURCHYARD
AND 164 PICCADILLY
1892

INTRODUCTION

I ACCEDE with great pleasure to the request of Mr. Morris that I should be associated with him in this book, which describes the journey which we took together, and conveys the conclusions on matters of supreme importance which concurrently we reached.

There is room for a variety of works describing other lands and other peoples. The works of those long resident in foreign lands who have made a calm and complete study of all they have seen, carry of necessity the highest authority, and are charged with elements of deeper interest. But it is obvious that part of what is gained in force is lost in freshness. By the time they write, they are so accustomed to the usages of the people that they have ceased to feel, and cannot therefore communicate, an interest in what at first struck them as so peculiar. The first impression has its own judicial value. There is, therefore, room for the work of those who write what they see, when they see it, with all the freshness of their own surprise.

Such is the special quality of the letters which are here presented to the reader. They interested a very large circle of readers from time to time during our journey, and they will, I doubt not, extend and deepen that interest; for they deal with varied themes, some of them the most interesting that the devout Christian can ponder. It fell to our lot, for instance, to see in the Sandwich Islands how much barbarism the Gospel could convert; and the respective merits of the progress created by the Gospel and the progress created by mere civilization could be studied side by side. In Japan we were permitted to mark how the Gospel could lay hold on a mobile, artistic, but withal sensual people, and commend itself to thousands as the best guide for nations and for men; while in China all sorts of questions of keenest interest met us at every turn. The sociologist, the geologist, the student of history, the student of comparative religion, the statesman, the Christian—all find there a field replete with interest. So that we had opportunities enough of seeing numbers of things, all new and of deepest interest.

Every reader of these letters will see at once that Mr. Morris is a careful and shrewd observer of all that comes within his ken. I can testify to his extreme solicitude to verify his facts, and to give above all things the exact truth concerning that of which he writes.

I trust that China as here disclosed will engage the deepest interest of Christian hearts. Containing one-third of mankind, united for ages by a common government, literature, and religion, it presents the largest single community lying outside the empire of Christ. Yet though through thousands of years China has lived an imperial hermit amongst the nations of the world, there never seems to have been a period in which she was not ready to receive new ideas.

Dr. Edkins points out in one direction traces of the Zoroastrianism of Persia, in the universal recognition of a principle of Dualism as pervading all things. India gave Buddhism to China. In Central Asia one section of Buddhism adopted from Mediæval Catholic missions a great many papal usages and things, amongst them an infallible pope—the Grand Lama of Thibet, whose sway extends over tens of thousands of monks in this land. The worship of Amita Buddha in Japan, Mid-China, and in some of the sects of North China, has elements which must have come from a Christian source. The doctrine of transmigration is held as keenly as by the disciples of Pythagoras 2400 years ago, while a survival of an ancient theism still gives peculiar sanctity to the Altar of Heaven at Peking.

What the conversion of a nation of such strength to the Gospel would mean for mankind it is impossible to imagine. But it is an event of little less moment than the conversion of Europe has proved. That they will accept the Gospel was impressed most profoundly on the mind of Mr. Morris and myself by many things : such as the aching void caused by the absence of all higher religious faith ; the spiritual eagerness for light shown by some of the more religious of the secret sects ; the lack of motive-power in the dominant Confucianism ; the benign services rendered by all the missions, and valued by the people ; and the great success that has already

attended almost all Christian missions both in the
north and south of that great empire. At the present
moment our attention is held acutely by the popular
commotions which have risen against the missionaries in the Yang-tze Valley. Whether they will prove
political rebellions, or merely religious persecutions,
time only will show.

It is deeply to be lamented that the doctrine of
transubstantiation should have been carried to China.
To the people there it suggests that Christians are
cannibals ; and they see in the numerous orphanages
which Roman Catholic piety has established throughout the land, only the means of supplying the Lord's
Table with the revolting meal. Such awful misconceptions render the work of the Christian Church
in securing foothold there immensely difficult. It is
to be regretted also that the undue patronage of
Roman Catholic missions by France, and an over-
readiness on the part of the Roman Catholic missions
to appeal to Treaty rights, and to carry things with
a high hand, has awakened dislike amongst the
official classes almost as strong as that aroused by
the misconceptions of the people. It is further deeply
to be lamented that as a people we are identified
with the nefarious opium traffic, which, finding a great
nation free from the opium vice, has so inoculated
them with it that we have developed a vice as awful
as drunkenness, and as common among the four
hundred millions of China as drunkenness is amongst
our thirty-eight millions at home !

But, in spite of all these things, Truth never faileth :
and Love never faileth : and the beauty of the Gospel

teaching, the splendour of its consolations, its sufficiency to give deepest peace and to quicken purest love,—all impress the people profoundly. So that in a little over forty years the half-dozen converts whom Dr. Legge found in China when he went have become nearly forty thousand. And these converts enjoy the respect of the missionaries (the best judges) for their constancy in the midst of persecution, and their purity and integrity in the midst of abounding temptation.

We went out fairly well informed of the statistics of Christian missions ; but we were not prepared to find such a measure of success as both in north and south, in our own and in other missions, we were permitted to behold. Shall we pursue this task to the complete success with which God waits to crown the earnest labour of all who work for Him there, or shall our hearts be feeble and our hands be slack ?

It were greatly to be wished that in this year, which marks the centenary of English missions, there could be a revival of the imperial compassion which the grace of Christ works in every heart that yields itself to its influence. It needs to be recognized that work for others is *the* business of the Church of Christ, and that the best lives of the Church should be consecrated to the work that is most difficult. In the revival which the Jesuit Missions in the sixteenth century brought to the Church of Rome, the men who went to China were the noblest men that the Church possessed. They left their professorships in the universities of France and Italy to carry the Gospel, as they understood it (and some understood it well), to that distant land. Their success, their sufferings, their mistakes, their consecration, are all 'writ large' in the world's history and in the Book of God's remembrance. Why should our purer Gospel be unable to secure the consecration of those who are manliest and godliest in our Churches to-day? When the number sent to China must necessarily be so very small in proportion to the work to be done, we want those for the work who are fitted by nature, by grace, and by culture, to be *leaders of leaders of men*. Whatever enlarges men's understanding of the ways of God and of men, and increases men's power of understanding men, is of supreme importance in the training of missionaries.

What results will come of our efforts, and in what order, it is not for us to speculate. That great persecutions will attend any very wide success of the Gospel, is almost certain ; and the men we send out should be men strong enough to exhort men to choose Christ in face of death, and strong enough, if need be, to die with them. But beyond the troubles which will attend a wider success, there gleams the bright day which God's promise assures to us, and the infinite reward of all well-doing.

May the testimony of the following pages cherish a higher faith and hope in our Churches, and thus hasten the day when this great people will see and adore the glory of God as it streams on them through the face of Jesus Christ !

RICHARD GLOVER.

AUTHOR'S PREFACE

THE question of sending out a deputation to China had long been considered by the committee of the Baptist Missionary Society, and our missionaries in China had been long asking that a deputation should be sent. 'Our work,' they said, 'has been criticized by those who have never seen it, and who have known little or nothing of the circumstances in which and the conditions under which that work is being carried on. Our work has never been described but by ourselves, and there are many who think, and some who say, that we are not the fittest people to estimate the value of our own work. Send out, then, two men in whom you have confidence, and in whom we shall have confidence. Let them visit our stations and see our work with their own eyes, and on their return give a faithful, unbiassed report of what they have seen and heard. With that report, whatever may be its character, we shall be satisfied, and we trust you will be satisfied.'

The request was felt to be reasonable, but it was one which could not be easily complied with. In 1890, however, the committee felt that a deputation ought to be sent out without further delay, and Dr. Glover and myself were asked to undertake the work. For myself, I may say that I never entered upon any work with more hesitation and reluctance; but there is now scarcely any part of my life upon which I look back with feelings of greater satisfaction. I am thankful, and ever shall be thankful, that I have been permitted to see something of that great work which God is carrying on in China.

Our instructions were to visit our own missionary stations in the two provinces of Shantung and Shansi, and report upon the work done. Further, we were to see all that could be seen of the work of other societies in those parts of China which we might visit. During our brief stay in that great empire we had the opportunity of inspecting the work of many missionary societies, and we were constantly moved to thank God for what we saw. We had read about missions in China, we had heard about them, and we were not disappointed when we were brought face to face with them; for extent, character, and worth they far exceeded our largest expectations; and so far from feeling that we had been deluded by exaggerated, extravagant, or garbled statements, we felt, as we passed from one mission station to another, that 'the half had not been told.' Again and again have we said to missionary brethren as they have quietly unfolded to us the extent and results of the work in which they were engaged, 'Why have you not told us this at home? It has all the charm of a romance.'

The account of our visit which appears in this volume was sent home in the form of letters to the *East Anglian Daily Times* and *Freeman.* These letters were written in haste, and under circumstances not very favourable to literary composition—on steamers,

Chinese river-boats, amid all the dirt and discomfort of Chinese inns. They recorded, from time to time, impressions made upon me by what I saw and heard. We travelled for the most part in the interior, visiting places which have never been visited save by the missionary, wearing Chinese clothes, living with the missionaries as they live, moving about in Chinese conveyances with them in their work, mixing freely with the people among whom they labour—and we were able thus to form some idea of the nature and value, difficulties and encouragements, of their work.

From the time we left Tien-tsin until we came on our return journey to Peking, we did not meet with a single foreigner except the missionaries. It will be seen from the following pages that missionaries in the interior do not live easy, self-indulgent lives. They are not Sybarites, living in luxury by day and sleeping on beds of rose-leaves by night. Their work is hard, oftentimes trying to faith and patience. Many of them have to work on for many months without intercourse with foreigners, and in the presence of great forces of heathenism with which they feel in themselves little able to deal.

The letters indicate the many serious difficulties and inconveniences of Chinese travel ; but the reader will kindly remember two things : the one, that in our journeying everything was done that could be done by our missionary friends to mitigate our sufferings, and so it came to pass that, through their thoughtful kindness and constant attention, we travelled with much less discomfort than that which they ordinarily experience, and of which they never complain. The other is the fact that we made our journey in the winter. We had to safeguard ourselves against the cold, which was often extreme ; but for a variety of reasons, which need not be specified; the cold of winter is, by the foreigner travelling in China, generally much preferred to the heat of summer.

We were nearly five months in the interior, travelling by cart, wheel-barrow, mule-litter, and other strange conveyances not less than 1800 miles. We moved at the rate of not more, often considerably less, than three miles an hour, the roads in many places being in such a condition that it was to us a matter of surprise not so much that we moved slowly, as that we moved at all. In addition to this, we travelled by coast and river steamers and Chinese boats more than 3000 miles. We spent most of our time in the three great provinces of Chih-li, Shantung, and Shansi, but we paid passing visits to six other provinces, and we saw the larger number of the treaty ports.

As a deputation from an important Missionary Society, we enjoyed great advantages which would not otherwise have fallen to our lot. Everywhere we met with a most hearty welcome and abounding hospitality, and friends connected with different missions in China, both American and European, freely placed at our disposal the information we were seeking to obtain, and sought in every possible way to aid us in our work. And this opportunity is taken of publicly expressing our thanks for the great kindness which was shown to us by missionary and other friends, not only while we were in China, but also in our journey to and fro. We would also express our obligations to the two anonymous friends who so generously defrayed the entire cost of the special mission which is here described.

With regard to China, I have sought faithfully to describe what I saw, adding only this word of caution —that any description of China and of Chinese life and manners must be judged strictly in relation to that part of China which is professedly described. The China of the ports is altogether different from the China of the interior. Northern and Southern China, Central China, Eastern and Western China, each has its own distinguishing features and peculiarities ; and a description which may be fairly accurate as applied to one district would be grossly inaccurate if applied to another.

In the supplementary chapters an endeavour has been made to furnish, in compendious and unpretentious form, information as to some of those things concerning which the deputation have been most frequently questioned since their return. Should the curiosity of any reader be stimulated by the little that is said, additional information is easily obtainable by those who may wish to make a study of any special subject.

These letters having been hastily written and sent home without any idea of republication, the author regrets that he has not been able to give references to the particular authorities and sources of information on which he depended at the time.

If what is written serve to awaken or deepen interest in China and the work of God in that great empire, the writer will be ever thankful.

MAP OF THAT PART OF CHINA VISITED BY DR. GLOVER AND
THE REV. T. M. MORRIS.

TABLE OF CONTENTS

B

CHAPTER V.

CHOW-PING.

CHAPTER VI.

CHI-NAN-FU.

CHAPTER VII.

THE GREAT PLAIN OF CHINA.

CHAPTER VIII.

T'AI-YUEN-FU.

CHAPTER IX.

PEKING.

CHAPTER X.

AN INTERVIEW WITH LI-HUNG-CHANG.

CHAPTER XI.

SHANGHAI.

A

WINTER IN NORTH CHINA

———•◦•———

CHAPTER I.

FROM SAN FRANCISCO TO YOKOHAMA.

Chinese population in California—China-town—Mission work—Prohibitive legislation—The Pacific voyage—Reasons for calling at
the Sandwich Islands—Honolulu—Marvellous change in these
islands since their discovery by Captain Cook—Yokohama—
Tokyo—The Pagoda of Towers—Shiba and its temples—Zojyoji—
Vries Island—Kobe and Hiogo—Sunday in Kobe—Mission work
—Productions—Civilization.

I PASS over, without remark, our pleasant Atlantic
voyage, and our rapid run across the American
continent, in which we saw just enough of that
wonderful country to awaken the desire to see more.
The only matter on which I would touch, as related
to the errand on which we were going forth, is the
short visit we paid to what is called China-town. In
the State of California there is a Chinese population
of 35,000, and of these more than 15,000 are resident
in San Francisco. These are all huddled together in
one quarter by themselves, and it is very difficult to
understand how so many people can contrive to
live in so small a space. This part of the city is

so exclusively occupied by the Chinese, that as you walk through its streets, and see all the peculiarities of Chinese life about you, you can scarcely bring yourself to believe that you are not in a Chinese city. But there, side by side, Chinese and American life touch each other at many points, not intermingling, but each retaining all its characteristic differences.

We called at the head-quarters of the Episcopal Chinese Mission. The clergyman in charge was not at home, but we had a pleasant talk with the matron of a female school and home, which seems to be doing a good work among Chinese women and girls, in a quiet and unobtrusive way. We were guided to this mission-house by a young lady, whom we encountered in the street, and who is working among the Chinese in connection with the Baptist Mission. The Chinese are creating a difficulty in San Francisco and all along the Pacific coast. They seem to be a quiet, sober, industrious, and pre-eminently frugal people, who can live and save money where others would starve. But they live by themselves as a distinct people. Their ambition is to save money and return to their own country, or, at all events, they would like to be buried at home. There were several coffins on board the ship by which we went to China.

The difficulty with the Chinese is a labour difficulty. They undersell the labour of the United States, and, in consequence, a very bitter feeling is displayed against them by the labouring classes, and this feeling is so decided and widespread that it has secured legislative interference. The entrance of Chinese labour is prohibited. The Chinese already in the

United States may remain, but no more must come in. The Chinese are not only a very industrious, but also a very persistent and a very ingenious people, and thus it happens that those who have the administration of this prohibitive law have need of all their wits to keep the Chinese out. Many of the most intelligent people I met with in these parts strongly condemn this legislation as unnecessary and harmful, and they did not hesitate to say that America cannot afford to dispense with Chinese labour. And in this legislation, which is designed to prevent Chinese immigration, we have another of the many expressions of the American love for protection. This prohibitive legislation has naturally excited a very bitter feeling in China.

On October 9, 1890, about noon, we went on board the steamship China, but our start was delayed until nearly seven p.m. It was a splendid afternoon, and though we grew a little impatient because we should not get through the Golden Gate by daylight, we much enjoyed the varied scenery which stretched away from us in every direction as we lay at anchor in the beautiful Bay of San Francisco.

After getting on board, we found we were not to proceed directly to Japan, but to call at Honolulu. There was a sufficient reason for this detour, which added several days to the length of our voyage. The China, on its way to San Francisco, ought to have landed at Honolulu a large number of Chinese ; but, having come from a cholera-infected port, the authorities would not allow them to land without subjecting them to a lengthened quarantine. The captain could not spare time for this, and so carried his Chinese cargo on to San Francisco, to be discharged at Honolulu on his way back !

We had about eighty saloon passengers—a few missionaries and missionary ladies, proceeding to their different fields of labour, a considerable number of Americans, and a few English, travelling for pleasure ; a good many Japanese, several Chinese, and a Corean gentleman, who had been acting as the Corean Minister at Washington, all of whom were returning to their respective countries after more or less lengthened absence from them. We were made to feel that, not Europe or America, but Asia, was the great object of interest to the majority of our fellow-passengers, for, besides those of the saloon passengers who were Asiatic by birth, or had commercial or social relationship to that great continent, there were seven hundred and fifty Chinese in the steerage. The crew was almost entirely Chinese, the servants Chinese and Japanese in almost equal proportions, so that we had an Oriental atmosphere about us, and received a Chinese education before we reached China. The more we saw of this wonderful people, the deeper was our interest in them.

Several of the Orientals on board had been led formally to embrace Christianity during their residence in Europe or America, and were intelligent and earnest Christians ; and others were deeply interested in the Christian religion, and favourably affected towards it, though at present, with several of them, it was chiefly an intellectual preference, they regarding Christianity as one of the most potent factors of our Western civilization, of which the Japanese especially seem enamoured. My colleague and myself had many long and interesting conversations with this section of our fellow-passengers, who were thoroughly well-educated men, and very conversable. They talked in a perfectly free and unconventional way, and with almost childlike simplicity, of their own position and experience, and of the light or lights in which our civilization and religion presented themselves to them.

The first Sunday service was conducted by my colleague. The congregation, though small—forty or fifty people—was a representative one, including many nationalities, and all seemed interested. Let us hope that the seed sown may spring up and bear fruit. The great Sower has many different ways of scattering His seed. The second Sunday the preacher was a Canadian Presbyterian minister; and in the evening, after dinner, we had a very pleasant devotional service, an American Baptist presiding, who had been some ten years missionary in Japan, and who was returning to his work there. On the third Sunday the author conducted the service, preaching to a congregation not quite so large as on the previous Sundays, owing to the almost suffocating heat.

On October 16 we approached the Sandwich Islands, our destination being the port of Honolulu, on the island of Oahu. This group of islands has been spoken of as the Paradise of the Pacific. It seems strange, looking upon what we see to-day, to remember that they were discovered only a little more than a century ago, and were then the abode of savages and cannibals. But so it is. In a place called Kanwaihoa a monument has been erected to the memory of Captain Cook—a plain obelisk of concrete —in the centre of a small enclosure surrounded with chains, supported by old cannon. The monument was put in its place in 1874, and bears this inscription:—

IN MEMORY OF
CAPTAIN JAMES COOK, R.N.,
THE GREAT CIRCUMNAVIGATOR,
WHO
DISCOVERED THESE ISLANDS
ON THE 18TH OF JANUARY, A.D. 1778,
AND FELL NEAR THIS SPOT
ON THE 14TH OF FEBRUARY, A.D. 1789.

THIS MEMORIAL WAS ERECTED BY SOME OF HIS
FELLOW-COUNTRYMEN.

As we entered the tropics, we were not only sensible of the increased heat, but we were struck by the intense blue of the ocean. In approaching Oahu we passed to the windward of the island of Molokai, the leper island, associated with the name and labours of Father Damien. The leper settlement of Molokai is maintained by the Hawaiian Government, and is well managed. They spend upon it nearly 100,000 dollars a year. There are seven hundred lepers and three hundred relatives and assistants of the sick— about 1000 in all. The lepers are not allowed to leave the place, and strangers can only visit the island with special permit of the Board of Health. As we think of the poor lepers who form this settlement, it is with feelings of pity and compassion, and thankfulness that as much is being done as can be done to ameliorate their condition.

The appearance which Oahu at first presents is not very prepossessing. Of volcanic origin, the mountain heights look drear and barren, but once round the bold headland known as Diamond Hill, the beauties of the island began to appear, and we felt that we were drawing near to one of those isles of Paradise of which we had often heard and read.

> ' I sailed beneath a burning sun,
> By coral reefs and isles of balm,
> Where orange groves and silvery palm
> By faint spice-winds were gently fanned,
> Until I reached a tropic land.'

The islands which constitute this group consist of Hawaii, Oahu, Molokai, and Kanai. In these the bulk of the inhabitants are found and the chief industries carried on. There are several smaller islands, which need not be named.

At Honolulu we were obliged to anchor in deep water outside the coral reefs, upon which the waves broke in long lines of surf. There is only twenty-two feet of water over the bar, and our ship drew twenty-four or twenty-five feet. Honolulu presents a very beautiful appearance, nestling at the foot of the mountains which form the background of the picture, and embowered in tropical vegetation. I was especially struck by the colours of the sea— every shade of blue—indigo, ultramarine, *lapis lazuli* —while nearer the shore there was an expanse of the most brilliant emerald green, and there, sweeping over the coral reefs, are the combers, as they are called, rushing over or breaking upon the hidden reefs, leaving only a comparatively narrow and tortuous entrance to the harbour proper, in which were lying two American men-of-war and many other vessels.

Honolulu, on the island of Oahu, is the capital of the Hawaian kingdom, the seat of government, and the great commercial centre. It is a town of considerable size, with a population of about 25,000. As we were lying off a considerable time—thirty hours—an opportunity was afforded of going ashore, of which most of the passengers availed themselves. Steam-tugs, sailing-vessels, and shore-boats were the means of conveyance.

The population of these islands probably exceeds at present 90,000. Of these there are about 20,000 Chinese, 15,000 Japanese, and 11,000 or 12,000 Portuguese. The Chinese and Japanese are largely engaged on the sugar plantations, the principal industry of these islands. The Hawaian nation has a complete system of national education, sustained by several grants from the national revenue, the total number of schools being a hundred and seventy-eight, with 10,006 scholars, mostly taught in English ; number of teachers, three hundred and sixty-eight, of whom two hundred and fifty-two are foreigners, and a hundred and sixteen of Hawaian birth. The public schools are free, while the private schools charge a fee of from fifty cents to one dollar a year for each pupil.

The Hawaians have their own postal system, which is said to be well managed—a telephonic system, which is much more largely used than in any European city of the size. There are over 1100 subscribers in connection ; the cost is very small. Railways also have been recently introduced.

Honolulu is well supplied with churches—Congregational, Episcopal, Roman Catholic, Christian Chinese. Some of the church buildings are of considerable size and architectural pretensions. The great attraction to visitors to the Sandwich Islands is, of course, the volcano in Hawaii, which for the size and depth of its crater has a place by itself among the volcanoes of the world. The crater is nine miles in circumference, and the depth varies from eight hundred feet to 1100 feet in different years, according as the molten sea is at ebb or flood. The Sandwich Islanders are nearly amphibious, and seem as much at home in the water as out of it. As I was standing on the deck of the tug which was to take us back to our ship, I watched for some time the graceful movements of a Kanaka boy, who was swimming about in the clear and deep water. A gentleman threw over a ten-cent piece; he dived after it and caught it before it reached the bottom, and came up with it between his teeth.

This week was marked by an incident novel to most of us—the leaving out of a day from our reckoning when we reached a hundred and eighty degrees longitude. So that we have had a week of only six days.

We were all anxious in our approach to Japan to get as good a view as possible of the Holy Mountain —Fuji-yama—of which we had heard and read so much, and it was somewhat a disappointment to be told by the captain that we should come within sight of it about five o'clock the next morning. 'If you wish to get a good view of it,' he said, 'you must be up very early.' I was on deck before daylight, and found that many of my fellow-passengers were already there. Our first view of this wonderful mountain, which by its form and beauty has so powerfully impressed the Oriental mind, was in the clear, cold light of the full moon, and a very striking appearance it presented in that light; but the light gradually became clearer and warmer. The sun at last climbed above the mountains on the other side of the narrow sea through which we were passing, flooding everything with its glory, and there rose up Fuji-yama out of a low-lying bank of clouds, in its solitary majesty, an immense truncated cone 12,265 feet in height, a height which is the more impressive because she sits there as queen, without peer or rival. No one was disappointed by the sight, however large his expectations may have been. Fuji-yama was more than all we had been told of her; her snow-clad summit glowing in the light of the rising sun, she was

> 'A mountain of white marble
> Steeped in light, like molten gold.'

The glorious vision soon faded from our view—the clouds gathered around her—and it was difficult, and at last impossible, to distinguish the sun-lighted mountain from the sun-lighted clouds.

We reached Yokohama soon after nine o'clock, but there was the usual tedious delay getting goods ashore, and through the custom-house, though on the busy landing-place, where we were waiting nearly two hours, we saw so many strange sights that the time did not seem very long to us. At last we got our baggage examined, and sent to our hotel, beautifully situated on the shore-front, commanding a full view of the bay, which is a very fine one. After tiffin, or lunch, as we call it, we chartered two jinrikshas, and after attending to pressing business, had a long and very beautiful ride, of about six miles, round by the race-course and Mississippi Bay, back through rice-fields, which were being cleared of their crops, pausing for a short time for a rest in a characteristic Japanese village, where we had tea in Japanese style, and were regarded with quite undisguised curiosity by about half a dozen young Japanese women, who stood round us while we drank our tea, chattering and laughing, taking up our caps and looking at them, and feeling the texture of our clothes. Yokohama is of considerable size and importance, and from being only a small fishing village in 1859, has grown to be a town with a population in 1890 of 80,000 natives, and 3737 foreigners, of whom 2487 are Chinese, five hundred and eighty-seven British, two hundred and twenty-eight citizens of the United States, one hundred and sixty Germans, one hundred and nine French. There are many marks of Western civilization— churches, schools, newspapers, telegraphs, railways. Yokohama may be divided into three districts—the settlement, the Bluff, and the native town. In the settlement there is the English Hatoba, the principal landing-place of the port, stretching away from which to the east is the Bund, some 1200 yards in length, where are the principal steamship offices, business places of different kinds, and hotels. It seems to be the principal promenade, where you see a crowd of jinrikshas, many people on horseback, and a few driving in carriages. If a lady is in the carriage, you will be nearly sure to see her handling the reins. With every carriage of any pretension you will see a betto—an outrunner—and these men keep near the head of the horse, at whatever pace he may be going ; he is certain to be there when the carriage draws up. The Bluff is a hill overlooking the town and harbour, whence many fine views are obtained, and on which have been erected a considerable number of good and pleasantly situated houses. The native town is of large extent, composed of low, slightly built houses—the open shop in front and the living-room in the rear, with the construction and general appearance of which all are familiar who saw the Japanese village which was a popular exhibition in London some years ago.

The following day we visited Tokyo, the capital city of Japan, and distant from Yokohama eighteen miles. We travelled by rail, and made the journey each way in about three-quarters of an hour. The railway is well appointed and well managed, and a large number of persons seem to be constantly travelling between Yokohama and Tokyo. Leaving the Yokohama station a fine view is obtained of Noge Yama, and on the hill is seen a large and somewhat famous Shinto temple. On our way to Tokyo we pass several towns of no particular importance, but within a mile and a half of the Tokyo station is the village of Ikegami, in which is a very famous temple, dedicated to the worship of a well-known Buddhist priest, Nichiren, who lived some six hundred years ago. The place, we were told, is of great interest, but we were obliged to content ourselves with a rapid and passing glance at it.

Tokyo is a very large city, with over a million of people residing in it. It is nine miles long and eight miles broad. The foreign inhabitants are few —in the official return of 1885 only one hundred and ninety-seven ; these have to reside in the settlement of Tsukiji. According to recent statistics there are no fewer than two hundred and thirty-four Shinto and 3081 Buddhist temples in the city.

On our arrival we walked some distance through the principal business street, and called on one of the missionaries, at whose house we met several others. On the way we paid a visit to a large Buddhist temple, remarkable, so far as I could learn, for nothing except that the empress frequently worships there. Having spent the morning in making what inquiries we could as to the progress of mission work in Japan generally, and Tokyo in particular, we bade adieu to our missionary friends, and under the care of our Japanese guide, started off in jinrikshas to a distant part of the city which we were recommended to visit, and we went through several miles of streets. Everything had a strange Oriental look, the people with their picturesque and many-coloured clothing, many not overburdened with clothing of any kind, but all apparently having something to do. The shops are so numerous that one wonders where the customers can come from ; and I may here say that these streets look more picturesque by night than by day—the shops, being

C

perfectly open to the street, have a bright and attractive appearance with their paper lanterns and illuminated signs. After a long ride through the busy and crowded parts of the city, we came to what is the official district, large residences and offices stretching along the river-side, the river being about as wide as the Thames at Westminster. We drove for some distance along the broad and well-planted road which runs by the river-side, and which we were told is a favourite promenade for the people of Tokyo on holidays.

We then returned and crossed the river, that we might visit a celebrated temple—the Pagoda of Towers—which we could see from the river walk. This temple, which is one of the most celebrated in Japan, is known by the name of Kin-Ryu-Zan, but it is more commonly distinguished by the name of the goddess, Kwannon Sama, to whose worship the temple is especially devoted. The representation of Kwannon is a small image of pure gold, only two inches in height; it is kept in the most sacred part of the temple, and is seldom seen by any except the priests. Besides the principal temple there are many subordinate ones, and a large number of different shrines and idols, before which you may see the worshippers devoutly kneeling. These shrines are so numerous that the visitor whose stay is brief gets completely bewildered by them. There are, among many smaller erections, a pagoda, an octagon building containing an immense number of idols, and a large hall for the performance of religious rites, and there are many representations of the miracles wrought by Kwannon, the merciful goddess.

The approach to this temple is by a long and broad stone-paved walk, lined on either side by shops, devoted to the sale of a great variety of articles, especially toys, books, sweetmeats, ornaments of different kinds ; and when we passed, this approach was crowded with people going to and returning from the temple. At the end of this walk is a huge red building, the entrance or gate-hall of the temple, while on each side of the broad approach are two immense colossal gods, protected by iron screens. They are the guardians of the gate, and are called NI-O (two kings). One stands ready to welcome those who repent of their sins, while the other welcomes the birth of an infant destined to become a good man. The visitor will notice in the courtyard of this, and, indeed, of all temples, a large number of tame pigeons. They are held sacred, and to give piously inclined persons the opportunity of feeding them, you will see women offering for sale rice and peas in small earthen pots. People do not visit Asakusa for religious purposes only, but for pleasure also, and pleasure of a very ordinary kind. In the temple grounds you will find a theatre, circus, archery galleries, tea-booths, shops, and an immense variety of shows, to which admission is obtained at a very slight cost. These grounds were so crowded that we had difficulty in making our way through them.

We now made the best of our way to the division of the city called Shiba, the garden of Tokyo. The roads here are clean, good, and wide, with trees planted on either side, and priests variously attired are met at every turn. The chief interest of this

district centres in its temples, all of which are probably well worth visiting, the most celebrated and
the one we were most anxious to see being the
Zojyoji. We reached this temple just as it was being
closed for the night, and we were afraid at first that
we should not get a sight of it ; but our Japanese
guide, who was a Buddhist, said he would try and
arrange that for us, and he went forward to interview
some of the priests, and came back with the announce-
ment that though the principal gateways could not
be opened till the morning, if we did not mind making
a little detour we might get in another way ; and so,
yielding ourselves up to the guidance of a priest, we
were led along in a way so tortuous that I am sure if
he had suddenly left us we should never have found
our way out alone.   The Zojyoji contains the tombs
of the Shogun, which are of great splendour.   It was
the custom to bury the Shogun of the Tokugawa
family alternately at Shiba and Ueno.   The remains
of seven lie at the former, and five at the latter place.
We passed through a long pebbled court, which contains two hundred large stone lanterns, stone pillars
about eight or nine feet in height, with an enclosed
space near the top for the light to be placed in : these
are offerings to the deceased by some of their vassals,
called Fudai Daimyo. Those of a much higher grade,
called Kokusho Daimyo, presented the numerous
bronze lanterns seen there, while six of large size,
and conspicuous as standing by themselves, were
presented by three princely families, called Go-San-Ke.
We felt almost like thieves and robbers, as with shoe-
less feet we proceeded in ghostly silence, and in

absolute darkness, save so far as it was mitigated by the light of the paper lanterns carried by the priests, and one or two paper lanterns of the temple which they lighted up. With such light as we had we could only see very imperfectly the wonderful contents of the temple, but we saw a little of the bronze and lacquer, gold, and silver work, which we should have been glad to examine at greater leisure and with a better light. After a busy day we just managed to catch our train and reach our hotel in time for dinner.

The next morning at eleven we had to leave for Kobe. Our first idea was that we should cross the island by rail; but when we found that this meant a tedious journey of twenty hours, and that while incurring additional fatigue we should save but very little time, we determined to go by sea, and secured berths on board the Omari Maru, and we had no reason to regret our decision.

We arrived at Kobe about four o'clock on the Saturday afternoon. Kobe and Hiogo together practically form one town of about 120,000 people, stretching along the bay, and at the foot of a range of moderately high hills, up the lower slopes of which the town creeps. As in Yokohama and Tokyo, there is the foreign settlement and the native town, with its unchanged customs and strange foreign and Oriental look—everything reminding you that you are in Japan—and yet, with all this, a wonderful intermingling of things imported from the West. Shops in which not a single thing is sold which would be familiar to a European or American, lighted with the electric light, and other shops in

which you would see a strange medley of things of
native manufacture and use, side by side with others
which have avowedly come from Europe or America.
After dinner two of the missionaries came down to
the hotel, and gave us a very interesting account of
the work of Christian missions in Japan, and one
of them kindly undertook to act as our guide the
next day.

On Sunday morning, soon after nine o'clock, we
started and went first of all to the Wesleyan chapel,
to see the school which is carried on there before the
public service. We were pleased to see a goodly
number under instruction, senior scholars all of them,
and we had a pleasant talk with some of the teachers,
who were very glad to see friends from England who
were interested in their work. We then went to the
native Congregational chapel, a much larger building, where a large Sunday school of adult scholars
was being taught. The children assemble for instruction at an earlier hour. This church interested us
as one which has not only a native membership of, I
believe, nearly five hundred, but is under native
management, and has, or had, a native pastor. They
are now seeking a pastor. We then went to the
chapel which has been built on the compound of
Mr. Thompson, the American Baptist missionary.
It has a native congregation, and the service was
being conducted by a native of great natural elo-
quence. We then hurried down to the Union church
in time to hear a great part of the sermon, that day
preached by a Baptist ; it is the church sustained
and attended by the English-speaking foreign resi-

dents, who, judging from that Sunday, do not attend in such numbers as they should.

Soon after three we went to the native Congregational chapel again, as we were wishful to see a real native service. The building, seating about five hundred, was quite full, and we were almost the only Europeans. We heard two addresses given with much freedom, and listened to with great attention. It was the communion Sunday, and we should have remained, but had promised to attend a meeting of missionaries at half-past four. It was a very enjoyable gathering for prayer and praise. Mr. Glover and myself were asked to speak, which we did very briefly, and one or two of the missionaries expressed their views in reference to their work, and their relation to the churches at home.

Our visit to Japan was so brief, and our opportunities of personal inspection and inquiry so small, that I do not feel able to say much about the position and prospects of Christian missions. There can be no doubt that a great and good and solid work has been done, the extent and value of which cannot easily be estimated; and if we inquire as to the beneficial changes which have taken place, there are but few well-informed people who would not be prepared to allow that Christianity has been one of the most potent factors in the production of results the reality of which no one can question, and in the advantage of which an immense number of people participate who do not in the slightest degree recognize their obligations to Christianity.

One great discouragement—and perhaps the most

serious hindrance to mission work—is the non-religious, or positively irreligious, character of a large part of the foreign and nominally Christian population ; another, operating in a different way, arises from the unreliable character of the native race. They have many estimable features of character, but steadfastness, sincerity, and truthfulness would not be reckoned among the distinguishing virtues of the Japanese. They are an easily impressible and essentially imitative people, quick to take up any new thing, and not reluctant to abandon it for something more new. Notwithstanding this, the testimony of the missionaries is that the Japanese Christians have stood well, and that, too, in the presence of opposition and active persecution.

The educational work carried on by several missions is extensive in its character, and, so far as we could gather, satisfactory in its result. We called at one educational establishment — that of the Methodist Episcopal Church at Nagasaki. There are two large schools, one for boys, and another for girls, in which they have had at one time nearly four hundred pupils, and we were pleased to find that all the pupils pay for their board, and, in addition to that, a small sum for tuition. The results of these educational efforts will appear in the next generation.

For many years the ambition of Japan has been to imitate and reproduce Western civilization. Foreigners who could teach them anything, or do anything for them, which they were unable to do for themselves, were welcomed. Everything foreign was popular ; considerable numbers of young Japanese were sent to America and Europe at public cost to learn all that they could learn, that coming back they might place their acquisitions at the disposal of their country. Since about 1888, feeling has been flowing more and more strongly in another and opposite direction ; there has been a strong conservative reaction. The cry now is, Japan for the Japanese ; there is a distinct and growing anti-foreign feeling, and instead of welcoming foreigners, there is the determination to get rid of them as soon as possible, *i.e.* as soon as they can find Japanese qualified to fill the places which have been occupied by foreigners. This reaction is affecting all missionary work. Christianity, which was popular as a part of Western civilization, is popular no longer, and while the cold shade of unpopularity rests upon it, fewer adherents will be gained, and some professed friends will probably fall away. I do not at all think that this is to be regretted. During the time that everything foreign was so popular, the success of missions was phenomenal. This altered tone of feeling will probably act as a salutary check to a too rapid growth, and prove a time of sifting, from which religious movements in the end take no harm.

Of the indirect results of Christian missions, I may mention the increased observance of Sunday. The Japanese Government have made it a public holiday. A great deal of work is completely stopped on that day, and in Kobe, while a great deal of work is going on, the difference between the state of the streets on Saturday afternoon and Sunday morning was as great as that discernible in some parts of London.

CHAPTER II.

CHEFOO AND TIEN-TSIN.

The Inland Sea and Corea—Nagasaki—Buddhist temple—Mission school—Fusan—Jinsen, or Shemulpoo, a Corean village—Corean funeral customs—Voyage to China—Chefoo—Yentai—Chinese filth —Chinese curiosity—Market gardens—Ancestral burial-places— Mission work—American Presbyterian Mission—China Inland Mission—Voyage to Tien-tsin—Taku—Railway-ride—Tien-tsin— Missionary work—Meeting of missionaries and mission workers— Flood and famine—Visit to famine villages—Extreme destitution— Chinese good nature.

WE left Kobe in a coasting steamer, making several calls at Japanese and Korean ports on the way to Chefoo, Tien-tsin being her destination. Our course lay through the Inland Sea. This sea is in its widest part some forty miles across, and in other parts very narrow, and we were for miles threading tortuous channels not more than one or two cables' length in breadth. The sea is not studded, it is in places simply crowded with islands, mountainous and rocky, always picturesque, and, except when we are out in the more open parts, thronged with junks, sampans, and fishing-boats of every kind. Some of the narrow straits through which we passed reminded me of the Kyles of Bute, and for hundreds of miles we had scenery far exceeding the finest parts of the West Coast of Scotland.

Our first calling-place was Shimonoseki, where we only waited long enough to leave and receive mails, and we then went on to Nagasaki, where we remained thirty-six hours. We arrived at Nagasaki about nine p.m. It was a splendid starlight night, and the appearance of the harbour—one of the finest in the world—was very striking. The harbour itself is about two or three miles long, and completely shut in by steep hills of considerable height. The town, with a population of 30,000, is built round the upper part of the harbour, the houses in places creeping a little way up the hillsides. When we arrived, there seemed to be a light in every house, while the almost innumerable junks and sampans each had its own paper lantern, the general effect being very striking. The next day we spent on shore exploring the native town, and visiting a shop celebrated for the manufacture of articles of different kinds in tortoiseshell. We had the opportunity of seeing the process of manufacture, which is very interesting, and many of the results, which are beautiful and costly. We paid a visit to a Buddhist temple, to reach which you have to climb some two hundred steps, and if there is not very much to be seen in the temple, when you get to it you obtain an exceedingly fine view of the town and harbour. After that we had a longer and more difficult climb up to the mission school, getting back to our ship, after a long day's work, at nightfall. At nine a.m. we were off again, and were thus able to admire the wonderfully beau-

tiful approach to Nagasaki, through which we passed
the night before when it was dark. We had a good
view of the rock whence two hundred Roman Catholic
Christians were cast into the sea, about two hundred
years ago.

Our next call was at an island called Goito, and
thence we made our way to Fusan, in Corea, where
we were able to spend some time on shore. There
is a Japanese settlement here of about 4000 people.
The Corean town is at some distance—too far for
us to reach—the road was so bad, and the sun
so hot, that we had to abandon our attempt. We
were everywhere followed about by a little crowd of
Coreans, who watched our movements with undisguised and childish curiosity. The country abounds
with wild flowers, some of them very beautiful,
and when the Corean children saw that we were
interested in the flowers they seemed to take quite
a delight in bringing the ladies of our party the
flowers which they gathered, so that we returned
to our ship quite laden with them.

At nightfall we set out for Jinsen, on the other
side of Corea, or as it is commonly called, Shemulpoo. There are really three towns here—a Chinese
town, with its characteristic features, a Japanese
town, and then, farthest from the landing-place, and
straggling into the country, a veritable Corean town,
in exploring which we spent most of the time at
our disposal. It consists of long wide streets, with
mere sheds on either side — rude frameworks of
unhewn wood, with rough thatch of straw, put
together in the rudest style. In almost every house

some work was going on, and in the shop, or on the roadway in front, some articles were exposed for sale. The Coreans are a good-looking people, with a peculiar and picturesque style of dress. The married men wear their hair worked up into a kind of top-knot; the unmarried men have it hanging down their backs in a very loose plait. They were all dressed in white, which they wore on account of the death of their queen, which took place about seven months ago. This mourning has to be worn for three years. I was told that white has become their customary dress, so that they are ready for a season of public mourning whenever it comes.

At Fusan a party of Coreans, one of them a noble, came on board our vessel, having in charge two coffins with the bodies of dead Coreans, which they were conveying to Shemulpoo to place in their fathers' sepulchre. They made a little shelter for themselves on deck, and during the forty-eight hours' voyage they watched their dead night and day, two at a time. For a certain number of days, at the commencement of a season of mourning, they wear a hempen sackcloth over their white garments, and a peculiarly shaped mourning-cap of the same material.

Corea has been only open to foreigners about seven years, and was known as the Hermit nation, so self-secluded was it. Owing to its position relatively to China, Japan, and Russia, it has come a good deal to the front of late. Séoul, the capital of Corea, is about twenty-eight miles from this port, and has, I am told, a population of 300,000 people. The Roman Catholics have a strong mission there, dating from the old Jesuit missions, and several Protestant Churches are represented.

We left Shemulpoo about three o'clock on Tuesday afternoon, and being delayed by bad weather, dropped anchor in Chefoo harbour at 11.30 on Wednesday night, eight hours after time.

Chefoo is a misnomer. The town of Yentai is the port to which this name has come to be applied ; while Chefoo is a harbour in the neighbourhood of Yentai, but has really no connection with it. When the town was first occupied by merchants of other nations, it was in the possession of French troops, and no foreign settlement was marked out The consequence is that no plan has been adopted for the arrangement of the houses of foreign residents, and they are mixed up in some degree with native houses. The climate of Chefoo is considered very healthy, as compared with other parts of China, and it is being increasingly used as a health-resort during the hot summer months. During the winter the Peiho is frozen, and merchandise and mails for Tien-tsin and the more northern cities are landed here. Chefoo is celebrated as the place where Sir Thomas Wade and the Grand Secretary, Li-Hung-Chang, concluded the Chefoo Convention, in September, 1876.

The native city is squalid and uninteresting, and is a place of considerable size, with an estimated population of 29,000. It is surrounded with a wall, erected in the time of the Taiping rebellion, and the gates of the city are closed every night soon after sunset. We saw a great deal of the native city during our short stay. The streets are so narrow that in many places you can touch the shops, which line them on either side, with your outstretched hands. In the centre there is a narrow causeway of stones very roughly laid, and on each side an accumulation of filth. There is a total and universal disregard of everything in the shape of sanitary precautions and arrangements, and as the Chinese seem destitute of all sense of smell, they live contentedly in the midst of odours which to an Englishman are almost unbearably disgusting. Yet, strange to say, the Chinese declare that one reason for their dislike of us is that they do not like the smell of us—we smell like sheep. The Chinese not only live in the midst of dirt ; they are dirty themselves. As a nation, they suffer from hydrophobia. It fills them with astonishment and dismay to see Englishmen use water so freely for purposes of ablution. The Chinese differ very much from the Japanese in this particular. There is a saying in these parts that it is as difficult to get a Chinaman into a bath as it is to keep a Japanese out of one.

The houses in the native town are low wooden erections, with an upper story ; the shops are open to the street. In them you see people working at their various industries, quite undisturbed by the presence of those who are looking on. In perhaps the majority of these shops—certainly in an immense number of them—you see people engaged in the manufacture, cooking, or sale of food. Many of the things offered for sale appear to foreigners very remarkable compounds. They are, however, eagerly purchased, and with evident approval consumed by the Chinese. These streets during the business hours of the day are crowded, people standing round the shops, some being purchasers, and more interested spectators ; the paved causeway in the middle of the street is thronged with files of coolies carrying burdens, and ponies, mules, and asses engaged in the same useful work.   Riding in a chair, it is often a matter of some difficulty to get along.   You see everywhere dogs, who seem harmless enough, though they occa- sionally lift up their voices in anger or surprise as you pass ; and pigs, always black, are constantly encountered, luxuriating in the abominations of the street, or, where there is room enough to allow it, lying by the roadside in lazy enjoyment of the sunshine.   The Chinese are as much distinguished for undisguised curiosity as the Japanese and Coreans. If you pause for a minute or two in front of a shop, you immediately have a crowd about you.   If two foreigners meet to have a brief conversation, they have forty or fifty people gathered about them, listening with as much appearance of interest as though they understood every word that was spoken.

Walking or riding in the outskirts of the town, we are struck by the diligence and skill of the Chinese as gardeners, and the amount of produce they get off small pieces of ground is simply astonishing.   This is explained by what they put into it.   Everything which can be used as manure is carefully collected and treasured, and you cannot go far in any direction without coming upon small heaps of manure, care- fully plastered over with clay to prevent evaporation. And you see as frequently other heaps that might easily be mistaken for potato-pits, to which are skewered down small pieces of paper with inscriptions. These, we were told, were ancestral graves—often of great antiquity.

Our conveyance was usually the chair carried by two bearers, a convenient and cheap mode of locomotion ; and by these we were carried up and down steep and rugged paths, where we should have been inclined to say two men could not keep their feet carrying a fairly heavy burden in such a way, but they are to the manner born.

Important missionary work is done at Chefoo by the American Presbyterian Church and the China Inland Mission, and, in addition to evangelistic work, there are hospitals and schools maintained, which are rendering valuable service. We had the opportunity of seeing something of both the medical and educational work done, and were exceedingly pleased with what we saw. We attended a native service in the Presbyterian church, a good-sized building, with a projecting wing at the pulpit end, in which the women sit, so that while they have a full view of the minister, they cannot see or be seen by the male part of the congregation. The building was well filled with Chinese men and women. The service was altogether in Chinese. The hymns that afternoon were, 'Just as I am,' 'My faith looks up to Thee,' 'Art thou weary?' and the Doxology. At the close of the service the ordinance of the Lord's Supper was observed ; there were about one hundred communicants. At the close Dr. Corbett told the congregation who we were, and what was our errand, and proposed a resolution to the effect

D

that they sent, through us, their thanks to English Christians for the interest they had shown in the evangelization of the Chinese, and their hope that they would continue to give them their sympathy, help, and prayers. The whole congregation stood up as a token of their acceptance of Dr. Corbett's resolution, and remained standing in token of their interest in and respect for us as Christian brethren who had come all the way from England to see them.

The American Presbyterian Mission has been carried on in Shan-tung for about thirty years. They have done a very fine work, and have at present a church membership of about 3000, and about 1000 candidates for church membership. The China Inland Mission is represented in Chefoo by Dr. Douthwaite, a medical missionary, who has a hospital and dispensary under his charge, and acts as local superintendent of the mission. They have also a large and well-conducted school for the children of their missionaries, and a sanatorium, to which missionaries can resort when a change is needful.

When we reached Chefoo it was with the idea, according to arrangement entered into before leaving England, that we should go at once up to Tsing-chow-fu, but we were compelled to alter our arrangements, and go to Tien-tsin instead. We left in a coasting steamer, which landed us at Taku, whence we proceeded by rail to Tien-tsin.

The line runs through a perfectly flat country, which was to a large extent under water, the result of recent disastrous floods. On our arrival at Tien-tsin, or rather the railway terminus, which is some distance from it, we found ourselves on the platform looking after our baggage, in the midst of a clamorous crowd of coolies, who were eager to act as porters, and we unable to speak a word of Chinese. While we were doing the best we could for ourselves, the Rev. T. Richard appeared on the scene, and saved us from all further anxiety. We crossed the river, and were soon under the shelter of his hospitable roof, our luggage following.

Tien-tsin is a large and important place, distant eighty miles from Peking. The city within the walls is small compared with the suburbs, which are of great extent, and in these suburbs a number of foreigners dwell. The foreign concession on the south side of the river is largely taken up, and is divided into two parts—the British and the French settlements. The Bund is a busy scene. In addition to business of a more general kind, immense quantities of rice are being received and despatched ; lying on what we should call the quay you can see from 100,000 to 120,000 piculs—the picul is about 130 lbs. The foreign settlement contains many good houses and business premises, and is managed by a public body, which has for its use what is called the Municipal Buildings—an edifice of some pretensions.

Tien-tsin is well known in connection with the treaty signed by Lord Elgin in a temple since called Elgin's Temple, or Elgin's Joss House, on June 25, 1858, and known as the Treaty of Tien-tsin. It made itself notorious by the cowardly massacre of the French Sisters of Mercy and other foreigners on June 21, 1870. The town is connected by telegraph with Peking and

Shanghai.   Its estimated population is 950,000 ; this estimate is, many think, somewhat too high.

The London Missionary Society, the New Connexion Methodists, the American Episcopal Methodists, and the American Board have here important, well-staffed and well-equipped centres of work, and we met, very pleasantly and profitably, with a large number of able and zealous Christian men and women engaged in the missionary work, some of whom have been labouring here for thirty years.

We devoted some time to the inspection of hospital and educational work, and we were much pleased with what we saw.   One evening, missionaries, mission workers, and friends specially interested in mission work were invited to meet us for conference at the house of Mr. Richard, and a large number responded to the invitation.   A representative of each mission gave an account of the work under his or her charge, and then we proposed a number of questions as to missionary operations in China, to which the ladies and gentlemen present gave replies.   We obtained much valuable information, and the meeting was felt to be a very pleasant one by all who were present.

While in Tien-tsin we had a remarkable and valuable experience.   The annual rainfall in Chih-li is twenty-eight inches spread over many weeks.   In July, 1890, between the first and twenty-second, there was a rainfall of thirty-eight inches.   Owing to these excessive rains a large part of the Chih-li plain was inundated, the water spreading with unusual rapidity, and of the drainage basin of the Peiho, estimated at 60,000 square miles, one-tenth part was completely submerged. Information is imperfect as to the extent of mischief done, but it is supposed that not less than 4,000,000 people will, until the wheat harvest of next May, be entirely dependent on charity. Imperial and provincial authorities and native benevolent societies are putting forth strenuous efforts to provide needful resources. The foreign residents in Tien-tsin, however, felt that they should take an active part in this work of benevolence, and they elected a relief committee, which issued a circular appealing to foreign residents in China, Japan, Corea, and the Straits Settlements, it being deemed inexpedient to send the appeal beyond these limits. The Chinese authorities assigned to them ten or twelve villages in the neighbourhood of Tien-tsin, for which they held themselves responsible. A deputation from the committee was appointed to visit these villages to check the official reports, and to ascertain as exactly as possible the condition of things, with a view to the early distribution of relief. My colleague and myself were invited to go with these gentlemen, and we very gladly accepted the invitation. The villages were divided amongst those who went forth. I was attached to a party which had to inspect and report upon two villages. Though the flood had subsided to a large extent, our road lay along an embankment, from which water extended in every direction, the villages being almost surrounded with it. In some instances the only means of approach was by boats. The country had the appearance of a great inland sea, the villages on slightly higher ground being islands or peninsulas, embankments here and there rising above the water level, and the courses of rivers and canals being marked by the sails of boats and punts moving in different directions.

I visited one village in the morning, another in the afternoon. I never saw so much wretchedness before. The houses—if such you can call them—are of mud, or sun-burned bricks, their internal dimensions would not be, on the average, more than ten feet square, about one-half of the apartment being taken up with the raised platform, the *k'ang*, on which they sleep, at the end of which is a small arrangement—like a copper-hole—above which all the cooking is done, and the flue running under the k'ang, the fire for cooking warms the sleeping-place. There was not then the pinch of actual famine, but it was within measurable distance. The people were absolutely destitute, and they could only be kept alive for the next six or seven months by the help which might come from without. No one who has not witnessed it can form any idea of the terrible poverty of these villages. In many cases, where the mud huts had been dissolved by the heavy rains, whole families had no other shelter than that afforded by grass mats supported by cross sticks or bent bamboos. The friends I accompanied visited some two hundred and fifty Chinese houses, and going as we did, with official authority, and on an errand of mercy, we had the opportunity of entering houses which at any other time and under any other conditions would have been inexorably closed against a foreigner.

It was soon noticed by our native friends that I

had a lame knee, and in consequence experienced occasional difficulty in the rougher parts of the road, and ascending and descending broken steps, and help was pressed upon me on all sides. Sometimes they almost quarrelled among themselves as to who should offer me an arm, and they at last took almost complete possession of me. I was a great object of curiosity, and there they were crowding and chattering around me like a lot of children. When they helped me up or down steps they uttered a funny little cry, as though they were lifting or lowering a heavy load, and then there would be a laugh, in which they evidently expected me to join. I inquired through my friend why they were showing me all this attention, and the reply was that having come so far to see them they did not mean to let me come to any harm in their village ; and when we started for home there was quite a crowd of the elders of the village talking to me in words which I could not understand, but which, I was told, meant that they were likely to perish from hunger, and that their hearts were full of joy that we had come to help them.

When we went to Tien-tsin, it was with the idea of going on to Shansi at once, by way of Peking. Hearing, however, that a large number of the representatives of the native church had been convened to meet us, we were obliged, after all, to go to Shantung first, as we originally proposed, and make the seven days' journey to Tsing-chow-fu, riding from early morning till late at night in a Peking cart. Mr. Harmon, our escort to Shantung, arrived a little earlier than we expected, and our departure was at last somewhat hurried.

CHAPTER III.

FROM TIEN-TSIN TO TSING-CHOW-FU.

Journey to Tsing-chow-fu—Chinese cart—Chinese roads—Chinese inns
—Discomfort of Chinese travel—Approach to Tsing-chow-fu—
Meeting with native Christians outside the gates—Cordial welcome.

IN prospect of this long journey, and with the view
of minimizing our fatigue and discomfort, our friends
made great endeavours to secure for us mule-litters,
or *shent-zus*, as they are called here ; but they are not
used in Chih-li, and none happening to be in the city
when we wanted them, we were, as some one said,
condemned to the cart.

Now, the Chinese or Peking cart, while a very
venerable and respectable institution, is, regarded as
a mode of conveyance, neither commodious nor
luxurious. It is a small but very heavy and strong
tilted cart on two wheels ; the whole conveyance is
built of very strong, tough wood, the wheels heavily
tyred with iron, and further protected on the outside
with iron bosses ; the axle-tree is of large dimensions
and great strength, and the axle projects on each side
of the cart some six or seven inches. On the bottom
of the cart there are several wooden projections, fitting

the axle-tree, so that it can be put forward or back-
ward according to the load carried—the same principle
as in an English dog-cart, though the altered position
is secured by lifting instead of a screw—and the body
of the cart, when got into position, is secured to the
axle-tree by strong ropes ; the shafts run through the
cart, so as to form the support of a rack in the rear,
on which heavy luggage can be placed, and to stop
the cart at a convenient angle when it is tilted up in
the inn yard or elsewhere.

The internal dimensions are two feet six inches in
width, by four feet in length, and the height is
sufficient for you to sit on the floor of the cart and
have a little space left between your head and its
covering, which is semicircular in shape.   It must
not, however, be supposed that the whole of this space
is devoted to the use of the inside passenger—if he
gets two-thirds of it he is fortunate.   Smaller articles
needed on a long journey are carefully stowed away
in the rear of the cart, and then one-half your mattress
forms a seat, while the other half is bent up against
the packages in the rear of the cart, so as to form a
support for your back ; and into this partially filled
cart you have to creep and get as comfortably seated
as you can, your feet extending so as to touch the
tail of the mule, and resting on a board like the foot-
board of our English carts, the centre of which forms
a leg-rest for the passenger, and the ends seats for
the driver and Chinese attendant.   Such were the
conveyances in which we were to travel some two
hundred and seventy miles.

We form quite a little caravan—four carts, eight

mules, and eleven persons, four of them English—our two selves, Mr. Harmon, who came from Shantung to conduct us thither; Mr. Farthing, who came from Shansi, thinking we should visit that province first, and who will remain with us during our visit to Shantung, and act as our escort when the time for our visiting Shansi arrive; our four muleteers and three Chinamen, who render us different kinds of service on the road. The mules are driven tandem; two animals could not run side by side through many of the roads by which we had to travel. There are rope reins, or guiding lines, but they are little used. The driver has a long bamboo rod, like a fishing rod, with a long, light thong, and he guides the mules with whip and voice. The leading mule runs two or three yards ahead of the one in the shafts, the reason for which arrangement soon becomes apparent: the mule in the shafts has its position determined by circumstances—the leading mule can choose its own ground to some extent, and so give help which could be given in no other way. Again and again our road has been a bog, in which the cart sank up to its axle, and the mule in the shafts would be over its fetlocks. The leading mule climbs the bank, and on firm ground pulls away, and so after much labour we get through on to dry ground again. No words can describe the feelings of a passenger in a Chinese cart.

The roads of China can only be characterized as bad and worse. I believe there are no good roads in China, except in the foreign settlements; all the others I have seen are unutterably bad. The very bad roads are, I think, on the whole easier to travel on than those which are slightly better. On the very bad roads the mules are obliged to move slowly and cautiously ; the concussions are very violent as you are jolted into a hole or jerked out of one. As the mules make a rush at a bank, and then without the slightest regard for your feelings, let you drop on the other side, you have your teeth nearly shaken out of your head and your breath out of your body; but then you have this consolation—that an interval of perhaps a minute must elapse before another such concussion will occur. But if the road improve a little the mules are inclined or persuaded to break into a gentle trot, and then every part of your unfortunate body is agitated by a constant and terrible vibration, and it is an occasion for both astonishment and gratitude that a complicated piece of mechanism like the human body can remain in going order after many hours of such treatment.

In one of these springless carts you start, let us say, at three o'clock in the morning, after a cup of cocoa and any little thing that can be quickly pro-vided in the shape of food has been disposed of. From that early hour you are jerked and jolted about till some time between ten and twelve, when you stop for breakfast and to give the mules, drivers, and yourselves perhaps an hour's rest, and then you go on again till six or seven o'clock, and as your day of solitary confinement and endurance draws to a close you say within yourself, 'Now will I take my rest in mine inn.' After some delay and difficulty you dis-cover the inn which is to afford you the much-needed accommodation. You drive through a narrow entrance, and find yourself in a fair-sized, often an immensely large, courtyard. As it is dark, you are not immediately impressed with all the beauties and conveniences of the place. The yard itself is a perfect Babel; the shouts of drivers and servants, the braying of donkeys and mules, the barking of dogs, confuse rather than delight you. Chinese lanterns are constantly moving about, perplexing instead of assisting your vision. You, however, finally discover that the yard is surrounded with low sheds, some of which are open to the yard, for the shelter of the cattle, and others of a slightly superior character, which are for the shelter of travellers, are enclosed.

You are at last conducted to one of these apartments. This is the guest-chamber, which has neither been swept nor garnished. The provision most commonly met with is two rooms about ten feet square, connected by a doorway, but not separated by a door; mud floor, indescribably dirty walls, an open roof with blackened rafters, and the reed thatch not always hiding the stars. The only furniture on our first arrival is a small and always very dirty table, on which stands a lamp of a pattern which dates back probably to the time of Confucius. The lamp itself is a small metal, shell-shaped vessel, with bean oil, in which is placed a cotton wick, the kindled end of which rests on and hangs slightly over the edges of the shell, which rests upon a support somewhat like a candlestick. But though the lamp is on its stand, it does not give much light to those who are in the house. Its illuminating power is equal to about one-half of an average night-light. We are extravagant, and light up two candles, which are held in position by extemporized candlesticks.

We have now to unpack our food and prepare our suppers ; and it would amuse our friends at home to see us do so. We live chiefly on the food we carry with us. We can get plenty of hot water to mix our cocoa with, and our other cooking has been done by means of a small spirit stove. Supper ready, we partake of it with good appetites and great thankfulness. We have now to think about our sleeping accommodation ; our Chinese servants, indeed, have been arranging for that while we have been attending to our suppers. In each room there is usually a contrivance called a k'ang—a brick or mud erection the length of the room and about six feet wide, covered with a grass mat ; on these, two on each, our beds and bedding are arranged. I ought to have said that though at first the table is the only furniture, seats are ultimately provided, out of respect for our grey hairs ; two arm—but not easy—chairs have been provided for Mr. Glover and myself, our younger travelling companions having to content themselves with trestles from the yard. In many inns nothing but trestles are obtainable. Before we retire to rest we have to consider our defences for the night against external and internal foes. The windows are paper, and generally need to be repaired, the doors very imperfectly close, and can scarcely by any contrivance be fastened against the active but invisible foes, rats and dogs, who may invade us in the dark watches of the night. We further take what precautions we can against more minute enemies.

One of our difficulties was to find our way ; three of our drivers had never been that way before, and the one who had, had lost all recollection of it, it was so many years ago. You travel for miles with nothing to guide you but cart tracks, and when you come to a place where cart tracks branch off in different directions, even after careful examination of their rival claims with the aid of a Chinese lantern, you do not feel absolutely sure that the direction in which you ultimately determine to move is the right one ; on several occasions we found it was not. We had in one journey to ford several small rivers, and were glad to find that we were able to do so. Two rivers we had to cross by means of barges. The most important passage was that of the Yellow River, which at the point where we crossed is a mile wide, and we had to go about two miles up the stream to get to our landing-place ; the carts and half our party were on one barge, and the eight mules and the rest of our party on another. Embarkation, dis-embarkation, and crossing took up about three hours.

At one town where we stopped for breakfast the chief magistrate of the district sent down to our inn two mounted soldiers, who were instructed to act as our escort till we reached our inn at night. They were well mounted, but poorly armed. As far as we could learn from them, there had been assaults made on travellers by bands of robbers, and hearing of us as a party of foreigners the magistrate was anxious that no complications should arise in the district over which he had jurisdiction. At the end of our journey we offered them a small gratuity, which they at first

hesitatingly refused, and at last graciously accepted.
They told us that they were instructed to go with us
or provide us an escort for the rest of our journey ;
but we assured them we had no fears, and were
unwilling to take them from more important duties,
and showing them our passports and sending our
cards to the magistrate with our compliments and
thanks, they did no more than get up early enough
to see us start the next morning.   The only misadventure we met with was the overthrow of the
cart in which my colleague travelled ; he was not in
the slightest degree injured.   This first journey took
us seven days and a half, and these were not short
days : we were on the road at three, four, or five
o'clock every morning, and reached our inn at night
at different times between six and eight o'clock.

As we drew near to Tsing-Chow-Fu, the thoughtful kindness of the friends we were about to visit
became apparent.   Two or three miles from the city,
several of them came out on their ponies to meet
us with two sedan chairs, to which Dr. Glover and I
very gladly transferred ourselves, and the luxury of
resting in which we fully appreciated after seven days'
jolting in the Peking carts.   As we approached the
city gate, a still further and most pleasant surprise
awaited us.   A large party of the native Christians,
who were then assembled in Tsing-Chow-Fu, attending the autumnal conference, came forth to meet us,
and bid us welcome in the name of the Lord.   After
exchanging greetings with them, they accompanied
us to our abodes, which we were very glad to reach,
and after a hot bath and a good night's rest in a

comfortable bed, we did not feel any the worse for our long journey.

I was very thankful to get back again to the kind of bread I have always been accustomed to. We took with us from Tien-tsin enough foreign-made bread to last us for two or three days, and then we had to content ourselves with native bread, which is steamed and not baked, and is like a cold Norfolk dumpling. The little loaves are called *momos*. They are rather larger than a goose egg, and very much its shape, flattened at the broader end, and have the appearance of small bladders of lard. Not knowing by what dirty hands they had been handled, we took the precaution of peeling off the outer skin, and then, hungry as we often were, we partook of them with thankfulness that they had been obtained.

CHAPTER IV.

TSING-CHOW-FU.

City of Tsing-chow-fu—Baptist Mission—The province of Shantung — Birthplace of Confucius and Mencius — Tai-shan—Buddhist monastery—Funeral of the abbot—Confucian temple—Hill of the Cloudy Gate—Buddhist heaven and hell—Intercourse with native Christians—Sunday services at country stations—Chinese food— Respect for grey hairs.

THE city of Tsing-chow-fu has a population of about 30,000, and, like many other cities we have seen, was evidently more populous and prosperous in former times than it is now. This city is the centre of the Baptist Society's mission work in this part of Shantung. It was commenced here in 1874 by the Rev. Timothy Richard, who was afterwards joined by the Rev. A. G. Jones. In the great famine of 1876–1877, Messrs. Richard and Jones, with self-sacrificing devotion, gave themselves up to famine-relief work, and, by the valuable and loving service they rendered to the suffering and starving natives, won for themselves a place in their esteem and affections from which they have never been dislodged. The famine opened up a way for the preaching of the

E

Gospel, and prepared the hearts of many to listen to and welcome the good news. Some of those who were first gathered in have fallen away, and yet a large proportion of them have remained faithful. This mission—subsequently reinforced—has been carried on with encouraging success. There are six foreign missionaries and seven native pastors, six of whom were ordained during our stay in the city. Work is carried on around Tsing-chow-fu within a radius of thirty or forty miles in seventy-nine different places, the foreign missionaries and native pastors being assisted by a considerable number of evangelists and other helpers.

At the time of our arrival large numbers of the leaders and elders of the native church were gathered for conference, and we had repeated opportunities of meeting and holding intercourse with them, of which we very gladly availed ourselves. They were a very fine set of men, earnest, simple-minded, strong in faith, and well qualified to render valuable service to the church with which they are associated.

Before, however, entering upon this it will not be out of place to give a little information concerning the province of Shantung. The area is about equal to that of England and Wales, and the estimated population is 29,000,000. The name Shantung means 'East of the hills,' as that of Shansi, which we are next to visit, means 'West of the hills.' It possesses a very large sea border, and is traversed by the Grand Canal, which furnishes, or should furnish, an important means of intercommunication. The larger part of the province is level, the hilly region being broken up into a series of chains of hills—we should call them mountains—running across the promontory. The longest and highest of these ranges runs with the general trend of the coast in Taingan-fu. Some peaks are over 5000 feet in height, but most of them are about 3000. The inter-vales are highly cultivated, and the soil generally productive, except near the shores of the Pe-cheli Gulf, where it is nitrous. Two crops annually are produced here, as in other parts of North China. The wheat crop is gathered about the middle of May, millet the end of August, beans and cotton the end of September. The willow, aspen, oak, locust, and mulberry are common here, as are nearly all the conifera with which we are familiar ; and I am told that silkworms are fed on oak as well as mulberry leaves. But the silk in this district is of a common and coarse kind.

Shantung is celebrated in Chinese history, and was the scene of many remarkable events previous to 2000 B.C. It was the birthplace of both Confucius and Mencius, and the Shantung people are very proud of their province. The high mountain called Tai-Shan, the 'great mountain,' is situated near Taingan-fu. This peak is mentioned in *Shu King* as that where Shun sacrificed to Heaven (2254 B.C.). This mountain is celebrated for its historical as well as religious associations ; it towers above all the other peaks of the range, and is set as 'an ensign among the mountains, and as a beacon among the hills.' Large numbers of pilgrims resort to it, and every religious sect is represented there by shrines, temples, and idols. During the spring the roads leading to the Tai-Shan are crowded with pilgrims, who in long caravans go up to the sacred spot, that they may perform their devotions and supplicate the deities for the various blessings they are supposed to be able to give to their devotees.

The people are very poor ; outside the cities and towns the country is mostly occupied by small peasant proprietors, holding on an average not more than ten *mou*, which would be about equal to three English acres. This land is held under the Crown on the payment of a small annual tax. The families depending on these small holdings are usually larger than English families, the patriarchal system prevailing, and in each family you would find ordinarily three generations represented. In a good season they manage to subsist in a state of what we should regard as extreme poverty ; when crops are destroyed by flood or drought, there is utter and hopeless destitution. I had some opportunity of looking into hospital and dispensary work, and I found that the most common ailments were those occasioned by the miserable conditions under which these people live. The men are many of them tall and well grown ; the women seem to be of an inferior type. They live in mud and stone houses of small proportions and of the very rudest construction, most of them consisting of a single apartment, or at the outside two apartments, and with little or no furniture except the mud or brick k'ang, and a small arrangement for cooking. The articles for household use and the implements of husbandry are the same in form as those used by their ancestors 2000 years ago.

We visited a large Buddhist monastery in the neighbourhood of Tsing-chow-fu. It is a very extensive group of buildings. We were very cordially received, and while we were waiting for the advent of the monks who were to conduct us over the establishment we were treated to the inevitable cup of tea. The monks have their heads completely shaved, and wear long robes of different colours— black, brown, and light grey. We were told that these different colours do not indicate differences of ecclesiastical rank, but the different kinds of service in which they are at the time engaged. We were fortunate in visiting the monastery when we did, as they were celebrating the obsequies of the head of the monastery—I suppose I may call him the abbot —who died about a fortnight before. The abbot is a very important functionary, having ecclesiastical jurisdiction over the priests and monks of an extensive territory. He was lying, or rather sitting, in state, in the attitude of prayer and devout contemplation. He was placed in a large hexagonal box, the sides of which formed a pointed roof, the apex of which was about seven feet from the ground. This was placed within another covering of the same shape, made of rosewood and other hard and dark woods, highly polished, with carved and pierced panels, richly gilt. A space was railed off in front, by which the general public passed. We were admitted within the rails, and allowed more closely to examine the structure. In another place there was a kind of temporary shrine, where a pictorial representation of the late abbot was exhibited, and the usual provision was made for burning incense before it.   We went into several different buildings devoted to worship, and one large building in which there was an elaborately carved shrine, measuring nearly forty feet in width, and I should think nearly twenty feet in height.   The monks were pleasant and intelligent men, with whom we had a good deal of conversation through our missionary friend, who acted as interpreter.   One of them inquired to what country we belonged, and when he was told we were English, he said he knew Mr. Richard, and asked if we belonged to the same religion, and seemed very pleased to hear that we had quite recently been staying at Mr. Richard's house.

We subsequently went to a Confucian temple—a large structure—in which were images of Confucius and Mencius, and a number of their most worthy and distinguished disciples.   There is nothing imposing about these edifices, all of which are noticeable for what I should call the three D's of China—Decay, Dirt, Dilapidation.   The idea of keeping anything in a state of good repair seems never to enter the Chinese mind.

One day we had a very pleasant excursion to a celebrated temple in the neighbourhood of Tsing-chow-fu.   It is situated on the top of a lofty hill, a few miles outside the city, named the Hill of the Cloudy Gate, so called because of a large gateway said to be cut through the hard limestone of the summit, though I am inclined to regard it as a natural opening, passing through which a magnificent panorama bursts upon your view.   In this temple there is nothing very remarkable, beyond the exceptional beauty of its situation, and some gigantic figures of gods and goddesses cut in the rock. There is also on the other side of the summit a cave of somewhat difficult approach, which we visited, in which is a large figure, cut out of the limestone, of the sleeping Buddha, his head resting on a pile of books. This Hill of the Cloudy Gate is about 1000 feet high. We went on chairs and mules as far as we could, and then I managed to scramble up the remaining few hundred feet, with the aid of two trusty Chinamen, who seemed pleased to render me the service. I may here mention a fact which will give some idea of the great difference between the night temperature and the temperature at mid-day in the sun. On Friday night my thermometer registered twelve degrees of frost in my bedroom; at twelve o'clock on Saturday we were eating our lunch in the open air, under the shelter of the rock on the hill summit, and the sunshine was so hot that I was glad to screen myself from it.

Another day we visited two Buddhist temples in the city. In the former of these I was impressed by some very beautiful inscriptions, which were translated for my benefit. In the porch of this temple there was suspended a large model of the abacus — which is universally used in China for purposes of money calculation—and the inscription over it was: 'Man has many reckonings; Heaven has but one.' And on two pillars which stood on either side of the principal doorway were these inscriptions: on the one, 'Man's goodness man despises, but God does not despise;' on the other, ' Man's evil man fears, but God fears not.' We then went to the other temple, containing a representation of the Buddhist heaven and hell. These are represented by groups of full-sized figures, which occupy the sides of a large courtyard, the symbolical representations being protected by a roof from the weather, and from the too near approach of visitors and votaries by open railwork, through which everything can be clearly seen. The first group represents the proceedings of a court of justice; and in all that follows you see in successive groups of figures the results of these proceedings. First there is a group who, judging from their countenances, may be supposed to represent penitence and piety; then a group of persons sitting down to the heavenly feast, under the form of a Chinese banquet to which they have been admitted; and then follow representations of cruel torture inexpressibly horrible —a huge cauldron, over which preside two monsters with human bodies, the one with a horse's head and the other with a cow's, while a deformed and hideous fiend is acting as stoker. Further on there is a woman going head first into the hopper of a mill, while a lean and hungry-looking dog is lapping up the blood which trickles from the millstones. And so on with scenes equally horrible; for one group representing heavenly bliss, there were, I should think, a dozen representing scenes of indescribable suffering. Another thing impressed me —that this was the only temple which I have so far visited at which any considerable number of worshippers was found. Here also as at every temple, whether Buddhist or Confucian, which we have visited, the priests and attendants have been ready to give us the information we asked for, and that with no expectation of a gratuity.

Our intercourse with the native Christians was most interesting and instructive. They are, so far as we could see, earnest, devoted, and simple-minded Christian people, anxious to extend among their countrymen a knowledge of the doctrine which they have been led to accept. In this district there are nearly ninety Christian communities in connection with our mission, representatives of which were assembled in Tsing-Chow-Fu at their autumnal conference. On the Tuesday after our arrival the conference met. On a later day six men, who had been trained in Mr. Whitewright's Institution, were ordained to serve the Church as pastors ; they are a fine set of men, earnest and capable, well qualified to do good work in the districts in which they are to labour. Dr. Glover gave the charge to the newly ordained pastors, while I addressed the representatives of the native Churches.

The first Sunday I went out on a wheel-barrow to a village called Ma-Sung-li-Chia-Chuang ; the journey took about five hours there and back. The room in which the service was held would accommodate about eighty people, and was quite full, some standing round the door. The service was introduced by the missionary who accompanied me (Mr. Couling), who acted as my interpreter when I preached, and in the intercourse which I had with the people. The natives were delighted at the visit of the Lao-mou-Shi (the venerable pastor or teacher), who had travelled so far to see them.   The next Sunday, accompanied by Mr. Medhurst, I spent eight hours on the wheel-barrow going to and returning from a village called Ying-tzu, the resident pastor being Wung-pao-l'ai, one of the recently ordained pastors—a man of exceptional devotion and ability.   After the service they told us that though foreigners did not usually like Chinese food they had heard from the city that the deputation had partaken of it, and that they therefore had ventured to prepare food for us, as a token of their esteem and gratitude, of which they hoped we would partake.   A simple feast was then spread for us ; and though I should have preferred the sandwiches we brought with us, I used my chopsticks, and ate the food they set before us, if not with a keen relish, yet with a deep and pleasant sense of the kindly feeling which they thus expressed.   At both these Sunday services affectionate greetings were sent from these Chinese Christians to the Christians at home.

CHAPTER V.

CHOW-PING.

OUR pleasant visit to Tsin-Chow-Fu at last came to an end, as all pleasant things must, and on the Tuesday before Christmas Day we were obliged to bid farewell to our friends there, of whose exceeding kindness we shall long retain grateful recollections. On December 23, we took our departure for Chow-ping, a two-days' journey, where we were to spend Christmas Day. I found the wheel-barrow so great an improvement on the Chinese cart that I resolved to use it again on this occasion, and one of the missionaries placed his barrow at my disposal. The wheel-barrow is one of the most important and useful of Chinese institutions, and is in this part of China more largely employed for various purposes than any other mode of conveyance, or, even of all other conveyances combined. Nearly everything is carried on wheel-barrows, and by the poor it is largely used to carry persons. Our missionaries have seized the idea of the wheel-barrow, and have improved upon it, and the result is that they have, for fine weather, the most comfortable conveyance that I have seen in this country, and one which, with its single wheel, can travel where no two-wheeled conveyance could possibly go.

The barrow is a strong wooden framework about six feet long and four feet six inches broad, with two short shafts at each end, which the barrow-men hold. The wheel works in a kind of slot in the middle, the upper part being boxed in. The wheel is a very strong one, three feet ten inches in diameter. In addition to the barrow-men, who are strong and skilful—as they have need to be—there is harnessed to the barrow, for a long journey or a heavy load, a pony, donkey, or mule. The animal is attached to the barrow by rope traces, about four or five yards long, so that he is able to choose his way, and can get on a bank, or to the top of a steep rise, and thus help the barrow-men as otherwise he could not. These barrows will carry two passengers, one on either side, or if only one, the bedding and baggage can be packed on the unoccupied side. The barrows used for conveyance of merchandise are very strong but rough constructions, and immense loads are carried upon them. On a long day's journey you will meet with hundreds of these barrows.

On such a conveyance I elected to make my two-days' journey to Chow-ping, and I enjoyed the ride, though it was somewhat tiring. I met with no misadventure, save that the barrow once overturned and rolled me out ; but as the ground was level and not exceptionally hard, the only inconvenience I experienced was the trouble of getting in again. Had the accident occurred elsewhere, I might have been thrown down an embankment or into a ditch. These barrow-men often choose what seems to the passenger a very perilous, though to them convenient, way, to avoid the rough road : they take the barrow-track on the top of a high bank—a track often not more than a foot or eighteen inches broad. You soon, however, acquire confidence in the skill with which these men do their work, and console yourself with the hope that, should the barrow overturn, it will be where the road is soft and dry.

Between four and five o'clock on the afternoon of December 24 we reached Chow-ping, and met with a warm welcome from the brethren there. After dinner we held a short service—their usual Wednesday evening service, which, of course, had a character impressed upon it by the season which was passing over us. On Christmas morning there were Christmas cards on my breakfast-table, and at twelve o'clock a native service in the chapel. After luncheon some of us went out on a pleasant little excursion to see a temple on a neighbouring hill, from the top of which a very fine view was obtained. We went as far as we could on barrows and mules ; the rest of the way I walked, with the assistance that is always so kindly given. On our return we found that the mail had come in—the great event in a missionary settlement in the interior. I need not say how glad I was to get my letters from home, having had—owing to the miscarriage of letters—no intelligence for three months. We had a Christmas party at the house of one of the missionaries, who provided a regular Christmas dinner, and except for the absence of those with whom we should so gladly have been, we could almost have fancied ourselves at home in Old England.

On the Friday morning we were off again on our journey—I keeping to my wheel-barrow—arriving in Kao-Yuen the same night, and putting up at a large Chinese house built many years ago by a rich mandarin at great expense, and now hired by a missionary at less than the rent of a moderate-sized English cottage. As in China every one travels with his own bed and bedding, it is not so difficult to accommodate guests in a nearly empty house ; a couple of trestles and two or three boards will make a bedstead, and failing that, there is always a floor to rest on.

We were detained at Kao-Yuen, at which we proposed to tarry only for a night, by heavy rain which lasted a whole day—the only rain we had so far seen in China. A few hours' rain renders progress impossible. The traveller is hindered not only by the badness of the roads, but by the unwillingness of the Chinese to expose themselves to heavy rain. As soon as the rain began to fall, we saw our Chinese servants busily engaged preparing their waterproofs— which consist of a sort of straw thatch, which gives them a very comical appearance, but which I am told very effectually throws off the water, keeping the wearer quite dry.

The following day we were able to resume our

journey, but the roads had become so bad that further progression by means of the wheel-barrow had become impossible, and I was obliged to engage a mule litter. It is not easy to give an English reader a distinct idea of a mule litter or *shen-tzu*. It is of rudest construction, and if the materials are at hand can be put together in a short time, and at small expense. It consists really of two scaffold poles, or what might be used as such. These are kept apart at a suitable distance by two cross pieces of wood, firmly tied by rope, the intermediate space being the framework for the body of the carriage, while the projecting ends of the poles form the shafts between which the leading and following mules are placed. The lower part of the litter is made of a network of ropes, hanging down a foot or eighteen inches below the level of the poles, while the upper part consists merely of an arch of bent bamboos, covered with grass matting. The packing of the litter requires skill and practice. Boxes and more solid baggage form the substructure, which is placed upon the network, and upon it is placed the bedding, so arranged that you can sit and lean back on the softer articles, which are piled up in the rear. The internal dimensions are if anything rather larger than those of a Chinese cart. The poles are attached to a strong wooden saddle with four legs—I can think of no better term—which keep the shen-tzu with the underhanging network just clear of the ground when it is off the mules' backs.

Into the shen-tzu you creep, and get comfortably settled while it is standing on the ground, and then, when all is ready, four men lift the poles of one end high enough for the mule to receive the wooden saddle attached to the poles into another wooden saddle already suitably fixed on the mule's back. The same process is then gone through at the other end, and then you are off; and in the litter you remain till it is lifted off the mules' backs again. This mode of travel is more restful than the cart; there is more movement, but less vibration, and there is little that can be called jolting, except when the mules make a sudden rush up a steep bank, or a plunge down one. The movement is peculiar, and not absolutely pleasant; it is movement on one plane—longitudinal, lateral, diagonal, in no fixed order of succession—and the result is that your whole internal economy is subjected to a constant and not very gentle churning process, and many persons are much inconvenienced the first day or two by a complaint similar in character and effect to what voyagers call sea-sickness. From that, however, I was happily preserved.

In such conveyances we set out for Po-sing, a good-sized place only some twelve miles distant from Kao-Yuen, but with bad roads, taking us a long four hours' journey to reach. Starting early, however, we arrived in time for the Sunday service, for which arrangements had been made, and which was largely attended by native Christians, many of whom had come long distances, notwithstanding the bad condition of the roads. The Sunday evening we spent in pleasant intercourse with the native Christians who crowded our room, finishing the evening with an English service, in which we did not forget it was the last

Sunday of the year, and our friends at home, who were spending it in the same spirit, but under very different outward conditions. The next morning we had another service, which was more largely attended than the Sunday one—a good many Christians coming in from neighbouring villages who had been hindered by the water the day before. That service over, we returned to Kao-Yuen, where we were to meet the native Christians the next day.

I here must mention what was to us a very pleasant incident. A gentleman of the city, a banker, who is not a Christian, hearing of our expected advent, intimated to our missionary, Mr. Drake, his wish to show his good feeling towards us by sending us in food, as the Chinese express it. The offer was accepted with thanks, and accordingly a Chinese feast was sent from this gentleman's kitchen soon after our arrival, of which we partook with chopsticks, the art of using which with greater or less dexterity you soon acquire. The next day Mr. Drake invited this gentleman and several others to dine with us, a Chinese repast being sent in from a cook's shop. These gentlemen paid us a complimentary call early in the afternoon of the day on which they were to dine with us, and we found them then, as afterwards at dinner, intelligent, well-informed men in many directions, glad of the opportunity of meeting us foreigners, eagerly receiving any information we could give to them, and ever ready to reply to the inquiries with which we plied them.

I should like to give my readers some idea of a Chinese feast, but I am afraid I cannot. The guests,

F

with the host, about six in number, sit at a small table about three feet square, on which there is no cloth. There is placed for each guest a very small wine-cup, and a porcelain spoon, in which is a small quantity of vinegar. Certain savoury morsels which are consumed in the earlier part of the feast can be dipped into the vinegar before the spoon will be required for the soups, which are placed on the table later on. When the guests are seated, after a few minutes' conversation, the host lifts the small wine-cup —or tea-cup, if tea is used—and, with a grave and slight inclination of his head, takes a sip or two. I may say the wine, which tastes like weak sherry and water sweetened, is served hot from a tea-pot. In the centre of the table are several dishes, or saucers, with cold preparations—meat, fish, and sweetmeats. The feast begins with sweatmeats—they form the first course. The host leads off, taking his chopsticks and striking them on the table to get the ends even. He then helps himself, and the guests imitate his example. The chopsticks are then laid down, and conversation resumed, or pipes lighted up. Fresh dishes are brought in, and so the feast goes on with much deliberation and cere- mony at first, but with much less of it after a while. It is quite in good form for the host—or, indeed, any of the guests—to take up and offer you some delicate morsel, dipping the morsel in the vinegar, should it need to be so flavoured ; and the portion which is thus graciously offered you must gratefully receive. The only way of escape is by passing it on to your neigh- bour. It also consists with the proprieties of life, if you happen to take into your mouth anything which it is inconvenient to swallow, to deposit it without any apology on the floor.   One thing I learned from these Chinese gentlemen, which shows how wonderfully this part of China is altering physically, that, a hundred years ago, Kao-Yuen was very much nearer the coast than it is now, the difference in distance being caused by the gradual filling up of the Pe-cheli Gulf.

The following day we had a very interesting service with the native Christians of the city and a considerable number who came in from neighbouring villages, more than a hundred in all.

About mid-day we set out on our pilgrimage again, under the care of Mr. Nickalls ; and as there was no inn in the village we were next to visit, we had to stop for the night a few *li*[1] short of our destination ; this was at one of the most wretched places at which I have so far stopped.   We, however, made ourselves as happy as we could, and, remembering that it was the last night in the year, I need not say in what direction our thoughts went out, or that we were in spirit present with our friends at home. We had a little service of our own, and though we did not sit up till midnight, having to start the next morning at four o'clock, to meet with a number of Christians in a village some li off, we, however, did not think it inappropriate to sing C. Wesley's New Year's Hymn before retiring to rest, ' Come, let us anew our journey pursue.'   Early next morning we reached our destination, where we found a large number of native Christians ready to receive us. We held a service with them, and had some very

[1] About three *li* = one English mile.

pleasant intercourse with them both before and after the service, and then pushed on again for our next stopping-place, where we were to be the guests of one of the native Christians, a man who is there considered a well-to-do farmer, with about ten English acres. He provided us with shelter ; we had our own bedding and stores. He also let us have some fish caught in the neighbouring river. The native Christians crowded our room, and kept us in conversation till it was time to retire, when we were conducted across the yard to a shed devoted to the protection of agricultural implements, at one end of which was a very rude construction, on which our bedding was spread ; and there we slept, thankful that we had a resting-place so good.

The next morning we were up in good time, as after breakfast we were to meet a large number of native Christians who were coming in from neighbouring villages to meet us. There was no room nearly large enough to accommodate us, and so we were obliged to have an out-of-door service in the courtyard. About a hundred and twenty were present. In the shade there was twenty-six degrees of frost, but in the sun it was warm and pleasant, and though the service lasted two hours, what with the sun and my furs, I had no sensation of cold. We had a most interesting service ; the length is to be explained by the circumstance that two addresses had to be translated, and I reckon that a quarter of an hour's address means more than half an hour when thus rendered. The Chinese, however, are infinitely patient, and you run a much greater risk of disappointing them by

the shortness of a service than of tiring them by its
length. On Friday we returned to Chow-ping, and
on Saturday we went to Chou-tsauen, a large commercial town of 80,000 people, in which Mr. Wills
carries on a useful work ; it is about twelve miles from
Chow-ping. We went there and back in chairs, the
double journey occupying more than eight hours.
On the Sunday, at Chow-ping, there was a great
gathering of native Christians, and our time was
occupied with them from morning till night.

CHAPTER VI.

CHI-NAN-FU.

A bonfire in an inn—Arrival at Chi-nan-fu—Good shops—Streets
crowded with wheel-barrows—The lake—Mahommedan mosque—
American Presbyterian Mission—Farewell to Shantung—Departure
for Shansi—Pleasant experience of Chinese respect for age—Chi-
nan-fu again—Refugees from Chou-ching-chou—Riot there, and
expulsion of American Presbyterian missionaries—Pang-Chuang—
Station of American Board—Hsiao-Chang—London Mission—
Welcome of unexpected guests—Perils of robbers—Missionaries
mistaken for robbers.

MONDAY morning we were off again, our destination
this time being Chi-nan-fu, the capital of Shantung.
We had two days' journey before us ere we could
reach it, passing through several cities of considerable
size. We were obliged to break our journey for the
night at a place which could only afford us the very
poorest accommodation. The one room we could get
was damp and dirty, the air freely coming through
the door and broken paper windows. Our 'guide,
philosopher, and friend,' the Rev. A. G. Jones, an
experienced Chinese traveller, said that the cold was
a trouble that could be easily dealt with ; the temperature could be raised, though at the expense of

darkening the atmosphere. With this assurance we left him to try the experiment. He accordingly sent out for a large bundle of kao-liang stalks (red millet) about as thick as your finger, and eight or ten feet in length, and with these he made a large bonfire on the mud floor. The temperature was speedily raised, but the smoke was suffocating, and we retired to rest with weeping eyes, which we were bidden not to wipe, as the tears flowing from closed eyes are the best protection against smoke. My bed that night was something like a five-barred gate resting on two trestles, with some kao-liang stalks spread on the top, and on the top of that a grass mat, and then my bedding. I have had several bonfire experiences since, but do not like the smoke. I prefer the cold.

We reached Chi-nan-fu on the Tuesday night soon after sunset. Our entrance was made with great deliberation, for the approaches to this great city are simply execrable. No more attention is paid to the roads in the neighbourhood of a great city than elsewhere, and the consequence is, that the traffic, if there should be a little bad weather, soon brings them into an almost impassable condition. Chi-nan-fu is a large and busy place, with good shops —what the Chinese would regard as good shops,— many of them crowded with goods of great value. Those who do not walk, ride either in sedan chairs or on wheel-barrows, and these conveyances ply for hire as cabs do at home, only they are found in much greater numbers, and serve you at much less cost. The streets of the city are literally filled with barrows, which are used for the conveyance of passengers and merchandise, and it is no uncommon sight to see one of these long, narrow streets blocked by two lines of barrows, reaching from end to end of the street. The immense carrying-trade of a great city like this is done by wheel-barrows, pack-mules, donkeys, and ponies, and men carrying burdens on bamboo-poles. The whole place has a strange, Oriental look, the articles which are offered for sale are mostly un-familiar, and the use of which you know nothing about ; you meet with continual surprises, and move about among strange things and strange people like one in a dream.

There are many things of great interest in this city, several of which we saw. Within the city walls is a large lake, about one mile in length by half a mile in breadth. On this we spent a little time. It is traversed by broad public water-ways, on either side of which are enclosures belonging to different persons, so that the lake is divided into compartments by banks, which rise a foot or eighteen inches above the water level. In summer, when these banks are clothed with waving reeds, and these enclosures with the leaves and flowers of the lotus, it must have a very pleasant look, and on the islands are summer or tea houses, to which the inhabitants of Chi-nan-fu resort in large numbers. When we saw it it had a rather desolate look, the only people there besides ourselves being a few men who were engaged in fishing and getting up lotus roots, which are largely used as a vegetable, and dried and ground to form a sort of arrowroot. We visited several Buddhist temples, one or two of them of large size. One of them is in the neighbourhood of, and in some way connected with, some remarkable springs, which throw up large quantities of tepid water with such force that it rises a foot or two above the general water-level, and the quantity of water is so large that, flowing through the north gate of the city, it supplies the moat, and forms a lake of considerable size outside the city walls.

While in Chi-nan-fu we paid a very interesting visit to a large Mahommedan mosque. It is a fine building, erected nearly eight hundred years ago, and is in good preservation. There is a large staff in connection with it—sixty deacons, nineteen teachers, and the chief mollah. The principal apartment is a very fine one, about one hundred and eighty feet in length by sixty broad, the lofty roof sustained by two rows of pillars, and the whole floor is covered by one mat woven on the floor. After the inspection was over, we adjourned to the chief mollah's private apartment—if that could be called private—into which, according to Chinese custom, the people crowded, filling every square inch of floor. There tea was served, and we had an interesting conversation with the ecclesiastics who were present. The mollah of the adjoining mosque came in while we were there, and gave us a most pressing invitation to pay a visit to the establishment under his care. This, however, we were unable to do.

During our stay we spent much of our time in company with the native Christians, and though we were the guests of the Baptist Mission, seeing much also of the representatives of the American Presbyterian Mission. The last evening of our stay

we had a social religious service at the house of Dr.
Neil, a medical missionary, attended by the mission
families in the city, Dr. Watson, of Tsing-chow-fu,
Mr. James, a member of the Society for the Propagation of the Gospel, who was staying at the house of
one of the Presbyterian missionaries, and ourselves
—the largest gathering of Christian foreigners ever
held in that city ; and we did not forget our friends
elsewhere, and the week of special prayer.   The next
morning we started on our return journey to Chow-
ping, where arrangements had been made for holding
a final conference with our Shantung missionary
brethren ere we set off on our long journey to
Shansi.

After a lengthened and pleasant conference with
brethren, in whose society and inspecting whose work
in different parts of Shantung we had spent more
than six weeks, we regretfully bade them farewell,
and set off for Shansi, leaving Chow-ping on our way
thither early on Friday morning, January 16, 1891.
One incident of our journey shows the respect which
is paid to age in China, and even such appearance
of age as distinguishes Dr. Glover and myself. We
arrived later than usual one night at a miserable
little village inn, where we were obliged to break our
journey, and on our arrival found the inn yard nearly
filled with heavily laden barrows, and the only guest-
room occupied by a dozen barrow-men. A lengthened
and rather loud-voiced conversation took place between
our servants, the innkeeper, and the representative of
the barrow-men, during which the mules remained in
the conveyances, in case we might be obliged to go

further in quest of a resting-place. The purport of this conversation was afterwards explained to me. The barrow-men were at first, and quite naturally, disinclined to give up the room of which they had taken possession ; but it was urged upon them by our servants and the innkeeper that we were Lao-mou-shis of almost preternatural antiquity, and that it would be a great shame not to offer us the best accommodation of the inn ; and they at last, recognizing the force of the appeal, good-naturedly turned out that we might turn in.

The sacrifice was not so great as the reader might imagine ; they were nearly as well off in one of the sheds as they would have been in the guest-room, which was a wretched place ; and we should have thought ourselves well off indeed could we have spread out our bedding on the floor of a hayloft or loose-box of a fairly good English stable. It was an open room, from which the cold could not be excluded, and for warmth there was no provision beyond the two candles we were extravagant enough to burn. My thermometer showed fifteen degrees of frost inside, and only twenty outside. The cold nights of which we sometimes complain are not, however, without their compensating advantages. We are not stimulated to engage in those entomo-logical pursuits which are the nightly occupation, though not the entertainment and solace, of those whose lot it is to travel in the hot season ; though even in winter one of the common and not most pleasing sights in China is that of the modern Nimrod, sitting in the sun by the wayside, divested

of his padded jacket and shirt, if he have one, dili-
gently hunting his legitimate prey, of which at other
times he is the unconscious or irritated victim.

We broke our journey, according to previous
arrangement at Chi-nan-fu, becoming the guests for
the Sunday of the friends in that city belonging
to the American Presbyterian Mission. When we
arrived there on the Saturday night we found considerable excitement prevailing, and that arrangements for our accommodation had to be reversed
and altered, owing to the arrival a few hours
before of a number of refugees from Chou-ching-
Chou. In this city—the largest and most important
in the province after the capital, Chi-nan-fu—the
Presbyterians have been carrying on occasional work
for some years, and they finally decided on establishing a station there, for which purpose they rented a
house as the residence of such missionaries as might
be sent. Tuesday, January 6, Dr. and Mrs. Hunter
and family and Mr. Neal arrived at the city, and
took lodgings for a few days at an inn, while their
house was being prepared for their reception. They
soon found that a very intense anti-foreign feeling
had developed, and that a decided and strenuous
opposition would be offered to their settlement. The
gentry and literary classes were evidently organizing
a movement which should result in driving them
away. The excitement increased, riotous crowds
assembled, which became more and more insolent
and threatening in their bearing, and at last a large
and armed mob gathered before the inn in which
the missionaries were, broke into it, and threatened

to tear it down. Dr. and Mrs. Hunter and their children, with Mr. Neal, had to escape over a wall in the rear, and find shelter in the homes of some Mahommedan neighbours, who treated them very kindly. They appealed to the magistrate, who refused to protect them, and while he would not tell them to go, told them that he would not take any responsibility upon himself if they remained. In these circumstances they felt that it would be wise to retire, and this they did on Tuesday, the 13th, just a week after their arrival.

We were all very thankful that they suffered no personal injury, though it is a bitter disappointment to them not to be able to carry forward the work upon the doing of which they had set their hearts. About eighteen months before, the German Roman Catholic bishop and his staff were driven out by a riotous mob, and their success on that occasion probably encouraged the natives to organize this opposition to the Presbyterian Mission. Dr. Hunter is a medical missionary. He has just published, at his own cost, in handsome quarto form, *A Manual of Therapeutics and Pharmacy in the Chinese Language*, being mainly a translation of Squire's *Companion to the British Pharmacopœia*, with additions from the United States, Indian and Chinese Pharmacopœias; and the work is regarded as such an important and valuable addition to Chinese medical literature that an appreciative and commendatory preface of some length has been written by the Viceroy Li-Hung-Chang—the most prominent and influential public man in China. It is sad and

strange that a man like Dr. Hunter, whose services
have been publicly commended by a viceroy of the
empire, should be ejected from a Chinese city, and
that he who would only be a benefactor should be
treated as a criminal.

On the Sunday night I conducted a service in
English, at which there was a larger number of
Christian foreigners present than had ever before
been gathered together in that great city of Chi-
nan-fu, and yet we could all meet in a single room
of one of the missionary houses.

Monday morning we resumed our journey, and
after further experience of Chinese inns, we turned
aside to tarry for a night at the mission station of
Pang-Chuang, connected with the American Board—
a society corresponding in character with that of our
London Missionary Society—and here, though we
arrived as uninvited and quite unexpected guests,
we were received by Dr. and Mrs. Porter, and Mr.
and Mrs. Smith, with that warm and overflowing
welcome which seems ever waiting for the wandering
foreigner in China. This station is situated in an
out-of-the-way rural district, with a number of
villages within easy reach, but far away from any
considerable city or centre of population. And there
is wisdom shown in the choice of such a ' location,'
to use an American phrase. In the early days of
Christianity the villagers—pagans—were the last to
receive the Gospel, and the great triumphs of Christianity were in the towns and cities. The very reverse
is true in China. The country people are not only
more accessible than dwellers in large towns, but they

seem more ready to receive the truth, and have much less to fear and lose if they should openly profess Christianity.

The next day we bade a reluctant adieu to our kind friends, and resumed our pilgrimage, moving slowly on till on Friday night we reached Hsiao-Chang, a station occupied by the London Missionary Society, most worthily represented by Dr. and Mrs. McFarlane, and Mr. and Mrs. Rees. Here there is a work similar in character to that at Pang-Chuang, in or near to a quiet country village, and with a large number of villages and hamlets within a short distance, in many of which evangelistic work is carried on with much success. The work in this district was conducted for some years from the Tien-tsin centre ; it has only been a residential mission for the last two years and a half. The Medical Mission work here and at Pang-Chuang cannot be too highly commended ; indeed, everywhere it seems to be one of the most important and encouraging departments of the great missionary enterprise.

This district is infested by bands of robbers. The night before our arrival at Hsiao-Chang a large party of robbers broke into a village inn, with lighted torches, guns, and pistols, and other weapons, and carried off some eight hundred taels in silver and other property from travellers who were staying there that night. There seems to have been some resistance, as several persons were seriously wounded. The robbers did not know that three Englishmen were peacefully sleeping in an unprotected village inn not two miles away, or they would probably have honoured us with a visit. On starting for Hsiao-Chang, we arranged to start very early in the morning, so that we might reach there in good time. To our surprise and mortification, we were not called till six o'clock, and, on inquiring the reason, found that the magistrate had sent word to the inn that we were not to depart before dawn, unless we went with a military escort, and as such an escort had not been arranged for, he told our servants not to call us before six o'clock.

Our late start was the occasion of an amusing incident. When we stopped for lunch we found that we could not reach Hsiao-Chang till seven o'clock or after, and we felt that the hour would be too late for a large party to drop in unexpectedly, so we sent on one of our servants on the spare donkey to prepare for our advent. On receiving this message about an hour prior to our arrival, Dr. McFarlane and Mr. Rees at once saddled their horses and went forth in company with our servant to meet us, as the roads were somewhat difficult and intricate. Having ridden out several li, they saw at a distance a Chinese cart, which they thought must belong to our party, and raised at the top of their voices a good English halloa, which they felt sure would arrest it if any Englishmen were in it. Instead of stopping, the cart went on at a more rapid rate, whereupon our friends rode after it till they saw that a mule, a donkey, and a bullock were harnessed to it, and they knew from that it was not one of our carts; they then left the cart to hurry on its way, they walking their horses leisurely back to the village;

on reaching which they found considerable excitement, the occupants of the cart having made it known that they had been chased by two mounted robbers, and the men of the village were turning out, according to custom, to go in pursuit of them. Our friends on coming up inquired as to what had happened. On being informed, they were able to quiet alarm by announcing that they were the supposed robbers, and everything ended in a good-natured laugh. This matter being satisfactorily settled, Dr. McFarlane and Mr. Rees went out on another road, and this time met us a few li from the house, where a most hospitable welcome was awaiting us.

CHAPTER VII.

THE GREAT PLAIN OF CHINA.

Its size—Appearance—Monotony—Poverty—Industry and isolation of
the people—The Hwang-ho—'China's sorrow'—Grand Canal—
Roads of China—Donkeys and pack-mules—A Chinaman inquiring
about the 'doctrine'—Approach to Hwai-lu—China Inland Mission
—A Chinese market—The To-chiao—A new conveyance—Multitude of donkeys—A pitiable spectacle—Mountain gorges—The
great wall of China—Loëss villages and inns—A narrow escape—
The province of Shansi—Mineral productions—Large coal-measures
—The Loëss formation—Richtoven's theory—Great productiveness
of the soil.

ON leaving Hsiao-Chang, our journey lay through
the northern part of the Great Plain of China. This
immense plain, which forms so large and important
a part of China, is made up of the united deltas of
China's two great rivers—the Yang-tze-Kiang and
the Hwang-ho. Its greatest length is about seven
hundred miles, and its greatest width nearly five
hundred miles, with an average width of three hundred miles, with a coast-line of nearly 1100 miles;
its superficial area has been variously estimated at
from 150,000 to 180,000 square miles. It is, for the
most part, as level as our own Fen district, and
almost entirely bare of trees. If looking across

the plain you see trees, you may be nearly sure that they mark the site of some town or village, or the margin of some stream, or some burial enclosure. In China burial-grounds are private, and are met with everywhere, and evergreen trees, such as the pine, arbor vitæ, and cypress, are planted in double rows round the burial-places of wealthier families. The graves of the poor are marked by nothing more than conical heaps of earth about the size of an English haycock. The naturally barren appearance of the plain at this season, when the wheat is only a few inches above the ground, is increased by the fact that animals seem to be freely allowed to nibble off the tops of the growing plant. The almost complete absence of timber in so large a district obliges the poor to use as fuel almost everything that can be consumed, and you constantly meet with men and boys and women with their baskets and bamboo rakes, gathering up every piece of millet root or dry grass that they can discover. Another illustration of the poverty of the people and the cheapness of human labour is the fact that you cannot go many hundred yards on any frequented road in this part of the empire without seeing men and boys with baskets and ingenious little five-pronged forks, eagerly collecting manure for the fertilization of their small plots of ground.

Travelling over this plain you are impressed, or rather depressed, by its dead level uniformity and monotonous and dreary appearance. The villages, towns, and cities, which are numerous, being composed almost exclusively of one-storied houses, and surrounded with earthen or brick walls, the exact colour of the plains, would not engage attention till you are close upon them, were it not for the trees, not often tall trees, which grow within them. The people inhabiting those portions of the plain which we visited were distinguished by what seems to an Englishman extreme poverty, and a quiet contentment arising from complete ignorance of any better conditions than those under which they have always lived. Hoping for nothing better, they are in constant dread of something worse—the famine which so certainly follows both drought and flood ; they are always on the very verge of destitution, and often suffering from it. They live on from one generation to another, with manners and customs that are practically unchanged. At each end of the village you see the public threshing-floor, and here and there in the village street the mill, to which the families may bring their little stores of grain, the mill being nothing more than a stone roller working on a circular bed of stone. In the interior it is more than ever manifest that the life of this great nation has been practically untouched by Western ideas and influences, save where mission stations have been planted. The natives round about these stations become acquainted with foreigners, whom they at first regard with suspicion and dislike, but who at last, by quiet acts of Christian benevolence, win their confidence, and even their affection.

The extreme poverty of a great part of the district can be traced to the frequent overflowings of the Yellow River (the Hwang-ho), which runs through it —a river which has earned the name of 'China's sorrow.' It is remarkable on many accounts, but especially because it has so repeatedly changed its course in its passage to the sea. In our travels we have had occasion to cross it several times, and in the ruined villages through which we passed had abundant proof afforded of its devastating power in the time of flood, though it flows along quietly and innocently enough in a dry season like the present. Rising in Northern Thibet, about a hundred miles from the rise of the Yang-tze-Kiang, it pursues its devious course for 2700 miles. It is known to have occupied in succession the beds of the Pei-ho, the old river, and the Ta-tsing-ho, the most wonderful change made being that caused by the great flood of 1853.

At this season of the year the river seems incapable of working much mischief; the volume of water for a river of such great length being small. The average width in the plain was not more than 1000 or 1200 feet, though where shallows and sand-banks abound the distance across would be two and even three times as great. The watershed of this river is estimated at 475,000 square miles; and in the rainy season when the floods from the mountains come down to a plain already saturated with heavy and continued rain, we need not wonder at the irresistible and desolating inundations which lay waste vast districts, sweeping away or melting down mud-built villages and towns, and destroying both property and life to an appalling extent. One cannot travel in the part of China in which we have been spending the last two months, without seeing that great efforts have been made to safeguard the people from these desolating floods; at immense cost and with immense labour vast embankments have been reared; but very little engineering skill has been displayed in the erection and arrangement of them, and still less care is bestowed upon the maintenance of them in good repair. Again and again, at road-crossings, I have seen them worn down nearly to the level of the plain they were intended to protect. From what I have seen I should be inclined to say that nothing is needed but money and engineering skill to save the country from these floods, which have so often occurred, and which, if things remain as they are, must inevitably occur again.

Before leaving this part of China, a word or two should be said about one of the greatest, and what should be one of the most useful, of the public works of the empire—the Grand Canal. This we crossed several times, and by the banks of it we travelled many miles. This canal was designed to be, and ought, at any cost, to have been maintained as the great artificial waterway of the empire, reaching as it does from Peking to Shanghai, and running through some of the most important provinces of China. But, like nearly everything else in China, it has fallen into a state of disrepair. The provisions for maintaining a sufficient supply of water are inadequate, while in many places the canal has been so neglected that navigation has become difficult and almost impossible. The shifting of the Yellow River from its old bed to its new has virtually intersected the canal, so that boats cannot pass from the canal to the river, or *vice versâ*, except at high water.

Owing to the absence of canal and railway accommodation, the more public and important roads of China present a very busy appearance. On the plain, wheel-barrows of large size, and strong though rough construction, are much used for the carriage of freight; it is astonishing what loads they carry. One of these larger wheel-barrows, with two men, and a donkey or mule, will go on day after day with the load of half a ton. I one day had the curiosity to count the wheel-barrows we passed and met; on an important public road I counted four hundred and sixty-five. There is no danger of a barrow passing you without notice. Every Chinese barrow has a scream or screech of its own; and a Chinaman would think it a sign of misfortune if his barrow did not thus speak to him by the way. To this four hundred and sixty-five you must add a considerable number that we should have passed or met in the hour and a half during which we and our beasts were resting in the middle of the day; and besides barrows there were many carts, pack-mules, and donkeys, and men carrying heavier or lighter burdens suspended from shoulder-poles.

Of this journey across the plain I have but little of interest to record. Day after day was occupied with a long and wearisome pilgrimage, beginning and ending in the dirt and discomfort of a Chinese inn. One pleasing incident occurred. At one place we learned on inquiry that there were three possible routes by which we could reach Hwai-lu, and as we were anxious to select the best, we took our innkeeper into our confidence, and consulted him. He was a fine specimen of a Chinaman, about thirty-five years of age, and seemed pleased that we should consult him. After he and our travelling companion and friend, Mr. Farthing, had been consulting the Chinese map, and had finally determined which road would be best for us to take, our innkeeper inquired if we had anything to do with the 'doctrine,' by which phrase Christianity is everywhere spoken of in China. On being told who we were, and what was our errand, he expressed a wish to learn something about it, upon which Mr. Farthing asked how it was that he knew anything about it; when he said that about ten years before a foreigner had stayed at the inn and spoken to him about the 'doctrine.' He could say but little about the interview; but it would seem that he, ever since then, had a wish to learn something more. The opportunity of doing so had at last presented itself, and of this he gladly availed himself, and he and our companion had a long and interesting conversation. We then handed him over to the care and instruction of one of our servants— an intelligent Christian man—who presented him with his own New Testament. Let us hope that, while the innkeeper helped us to find our way to Hwai-lu, the instruction he received during our short stay at his inn may help him to find his way to that better city which hath the foundations, whose Builder and Maker is God.

We at last drew near to Hwai-lu, and were glad to come within sight of the mountains again after the dreary flatness of the plain. When about fifteen li from the city my attention was engaged by the

most remarkable mountain outline I ever saw; it is
that of a recumbent figure of gigantic proportions—
the forehead, nose, mouth, and chin forming a perfect
profile—while another range of hills in the rear fits
in with an outline of the body, all standing out in
clear relief against the unclouded clearness of the
western sky. We had taken the precaution of sending
on one of our servants to announce our approach to
Mr. and Mrs. Simpson, who occupy that city as
representatives of the China Inland Mission; and
long before we reached the city gate we met Mr.
Simpson, who had come forth to bid us welcome, and
conduct us to his house. Whatever faults may be
laid at the doors of Chinese missionaries, no one can
say of them or their wives that they are 'forgetful
to entertain strangers.'

Hwai-lu is a city of considerable size, with a population of some 30,000 people, and it owes much of its
importance to its position, being situated at or near
the junction of two great roads running respectively
north and south and east and west, standing at the
very entrance of the great mountain-pass by which
we were to travel, and which is one of the great highways connecting east and west. Here for the first
time we met with camels, which are largely used
as beasts of burden, coming in laden with products
of Thibet and Mongolia, and going back laden with
the products of the plain. We were obliged to stay
twenty-four hours in this city, having to dismiss our
shentzus and muleteers, and engage what are called
to-chiaos (to-jios), a sort of sedan chair of large
size suspended between poles, like the mule-litters.

We needed to have both men and mules accustomed to the mountain-roads by which we were to travel for the next five days and a half. Reaching Hwai-lu about one o'clock in the afternoon, we did not leave till the same hour the next day.

On the morning of our departure, Mr. Simpson took us out to see the market or fair, one of the largest in North China, and exceptionally large on this occasion, being held so near to the Chinese New Year. The market is held on a plain, which stretches between the western wall of the city and the foot of the hills, which plain was crowded with an immense assemblage of people, many of whom belonged to the city, but the larger number being made up of those who had come in from towns and villages for many miles round. It was one of the busiest and strangest scenes I ever witnessed. Most of the goods offered for sale were spread out on the ground—immense quantities of goods of different kinds, articles of household use, which were nearly all strange to us—in fact, everything was strange,—and all this buying and selling was carried on with an amount of noise peculiar to a Chinese market. One of the strangest and saddest sights of the morning was a criminal carrying a heavy iron bar, about six feet long, and nearly as thick as a man's wrist, to which he was chained at the neck, wrists, and ankles. He could only move a few feet at a time, so heavily was he ironed, and how he could get any rest was more than I could discover. I had before this seen prisoners wearing the cangue—the well-known wooden collar. That punishment was bad enough, but this was far worse.

On Friday, January 30, we started afresh on our journey, using to-chiaos, which are decidedly more comfortable than shentzus, and though we at once entered upon a mountain-road, we were struck by the immense traffic which crowded and at times almost choked it. Leaving the plain, barrows disappear, and goods are carried almost exclusively by pack-mules and donkeys by day, and long trains of camels by night. The road is such that scarcely any other mode of conveyance is available, although a few adventurous carts find their way across the mountains. The road is often so rough, and the gradients in places so steep, that you wonder how any animal heavily laden can keep its feet. Donkeys and mules, however, are almost as sure-footed as goats. At one place where the road was for the time impassably crowded, my mules took it into their heads to climb to the top of a half-broken-down stone wall, over the uneven surface of which they carefully picked their way for a couple of hundred yards as complacently as if they had beneath their feet a good macadamized road. It was a satisfaction to me when they condescended to the lower and, as I thought, safer level. No effort is made to remedy the defects or remove the obstacles from Chinese roads ; the traffic is merely turned on one side till the road becomes useable again. On one occasion, as we were going along a dusty and stoneless road, I saw a large boulder lying before me, and I wondered how long it had been there, and how much longer it would remain. While I was thus wondering, my hinder mule stumbled over another and similar obstacle and fell, and my to-chiao came down with a great crash and shock, though without any injury to myself. Fortunately enough our party was within call to extricate the mule and set us going again; and it must be remembered that it requires five men to do this—four to lift the shafts of a loaded to-chiao, and one to put the mule into them.

We stopped the first night at Yu-Shui, and, starting the next morning two hours before daylight, we met and passed nearly four hundred camels; indeed, in places the road was so thronged with trains of camels passing eastward and westward that we could with difficulty get along. As soon as it was daylight the road was crowded with pack-mules and donkeys, three-fourths of them laden with coal and rough iron castings from the mines and iron works, which are found among the hills, the remainder carrying other merchandise. I amused myself by counting the number we passed and met in the three different hours during the day. The numbers were—three hundred and eighty-nine, two hundred and thirty-five, and six hundred and fifty-one; and the road was thus crowded for about half the distance to T'ai-yuen-fu; after that the traffic was very considerably less. We passed one pitiable spectacle—a man who in a fit of drunken frenzy had murdered six persons, several of them belonging to his own family. He was carried on a sort of tray, suspended from a shoulder-pole, by two men; he was firmly bound, and clothed in such a way as to show to passers-by that he was a criminal of the first degree. He was being thus conveyed to T'ai-yuen-fu to be publicly executed. As there are no newspapers to give information, we heard nothing more of him.

The road by which we travelled from Hwai-lu to T'ai-yuen-fu is remarkable in many respects. For many miles we went through loëss gorges, which form so striking a feature of this part of the country, the road in many places not wide enough for two Chinese carts to pass, while on either side, rising precipitously to a great height, are the loess cliffs ; then perhaps for several miles the path lies across a sandy plain shut in by mountains, then along some rock-paved or boulder-strewn river-bed, then through some mountain-pass as wild and desolate-looking as Glencoe, and every now and then we came quite unexpectedly on a good-sized city or town nestling among the hills.

On our way we passed through the Great Wall of China. This was not the main line of wall, but an extension or spur from it, designed to guard the mountain-passes of this Shansi range. According to Dr. Edkins, the wall separating Shansi and Chih-li dates from the time of the contending states, Chan-kow, B.C. 300, when the Chan kingdom separated itself from the Yen kingdom by a wall—Shansi was Chan, and Chih-li, Yen. Such strength as it has now is owing to the exertions of the Ming dynasty to keep itself in security against the Mongols.

This wall is the most remarkable of all the public works of China. According to Chinese records, it was finished two hundred and five years before Christ, and is said to be, with its extensions, nearly 1600 miles long. It is from twenty-five to thirty feet high, and from fifteen to twenty feet thick. At regular intervals there are turrets rising considerably above the level of the wall, and projecting some feet beyond it, commanding the face of the wall right and left. Passing through the gate, it presents a remarkable appearance, stretching away in both directions without regard to natural obstacles, now climbing the mountain-top, then lost to sight in the depths of some ravine; and then appearing again on the other side, and so it stretches along the northern and western borders of the empire, designed to guard them—and well adapted to guard them—against the inroads of the wild hordes beyond. That part of the wall which we saw had evidently been rebuilt in comparatively recent times; there were upon it no marks of extreme antiquity.

The winding mountain-road here completely boxes the compass, and the Chinese have built, spanning the road, four gateways, which are called respectively the Heavenly Gates of the East and the West, the North and the South. I shall never forget the prospect which suddenly burst upon us on passing through the Heavenly Gate South. It stands upon a mountain-summit nearly 4000 feet above the level of the sea, and on passing through affords an uninterrupted view of an almost semicircular sweep of country, the radius being not less than forty or fifty miles. The surface is strangely varied—there is a perfect network of loess gorges, hills, and mountains in every direction, some of them two or three thousand feet in height, with the loess terraces in many instances climbing to the mountain-top, and all this standing out with the

utmost clearness under a cloudless sky, and seen
through a transparent atmosphere.

It may not be generally known that there are cave-
dwellers in China ; but so it is—caves dug out in the
precipitous loëss cliffs, which provide homes for hundreds of thousands—some say for millions—of people
in this part of China.   These excavations rise terrace
above terrace, whole villages being made up of them.
Many of these homes are very miserable—a mere hole
dug in the cliff, with a grass mat covering the aperture
to keep the cold out.   But there are many houses of
considerable pretensions, the excavations being arched
with burnt bricks, and the fronts faced with stone or
brick, with properly constructed Chinese doors and
windows.   We several times lodged at inns formed of
excavations in the loëss.   Our experience one night
was not pleasant.   The guest-chamber assigned to
us was an excavation in the cliff, about twenty-five
feet long by ten feet broad, and about ten or eleven
feet to the crown of the semicircular roof ; it looked
exactly like a small railway arch ; the access to the
room was by the usual double doors, on each side
of which was a small paper-covered window.   The
ground floor was occupied by a k'ang about fourteen
feet by six feet, and another across the end of the
apartment, ten feet by six feet.   The only furniture
was a table placed between the two k'angs, and our
only seats the edges of the same.   The larger k'ang
was warmed by a furnace and the usual flue ; the one
at the end of the room was cold, and on it we elected
to have our bedding spread.   We hoped to get sufficient fresh air through the very obvious chinks of

the door and sundry broken panes of paper.   Several times during the evening we thought we detected sulphurous fumes, and sent out to inquire if charcoal were burning, but we were assured that only wood and coal had been used in warming the k'ang, and that its flue opened out somewhere in front of the dwelling.

With this assurance we retired to rest, and fell asleep ; but early in the morning I awoke with a strange feeling of oppression and general discomfort ; but knowing how valuable sleep is on such a journey, I was unwilling to disturb my neighbours.   Between four and five our servants called us, and on comparing notes we found that we all had been suffering from the same symptoms, and when we got up we were so dazed and stupefied that we could scarcely stand and attend to our very simple toilets.   With breakfast nearly untouched we set out on our journey, hoping that the fresh morning air, with the thermometer nearly down to zero, would soon set us right again. It was, however, many hours before I recovered from the effects of the *ch'i*, as the sulphurous smoke from the k'ang is called.   We had had a very narrow escape of our lives, and we were told afterwards that many lives are lost every winter in these ill-ventilated sleeping-places.   A very grim suggestion appeared in a native paper just afterwards—recommending parties of travellers to secure the company of an elderly man, who, being a light sleeper, will probably wake up before the point of suffocation is reached.

We entered Shansi a few li to the east of the Customs Barrier, which is maintained in the narrowest part of the mountain-pass, not far from the Great Wall. Shansi is a province of China with an area nearly equal to that of England and Wales, and with an estimated population of nineteen millions. The Yellow River bounds it on the west and partly on the south ; the Great Wall forms most of its northern boundary, while on the east it is shut off from the Great Plain by a range of lofty mountains. With the exception of two large stretches of table-land, some thousands of feet above the sea-level, its surface is rugged and mountainous, presenting a striking contrast to the vast plains of Shantung and Chih-li. This province is very rich in minerals, with large coal and iron formations. The coal is of varying quality, and the mines are worked in a very simple and primitive fashion. The supply of anthracite and bituminous coal is practically inexhaustible—indeed, experts have affirmed that the coal-measures of North China are the largest in the world. The two great plateaux to which I have referred are covered by the remarkable loëss deposit—a deposit which varies in depth from a few feet to five or six hundred.

For the following particulars as to this interesting deposit, I am indebted to Dr. Williams' *Middle Kingdom*, to which I would refer my readers for additional information. The loëss beds, covering a great part of North China, are among the most interesting of all geological formations. Attention was first directed to this deposit by Pumpelly (the American geologist) in 1864, since which time the formation and extent of these beds have been carefully examined by geologists, especially by Baron

H

von Richtoven, whose theory as to this deposit is now pretty generally accepted. The part of China more or less completely covered by this deposit lies between 99 and 115 deg. long. and 33 and 41 deg. lat., though there is reason for believing that it extends far beyond the limits of China proper in a northerly and easterly direction. This formation has been found in Shansi at a height of 7200 feet above the sea-level; it is also found in the Rhine valley and several other parts of Europe, but nowhere as it is found here. One peculiarity of the loëss is that its cleavage is invariably vertical. The consequence of this is the splitting up of its mass into sudden and multitudinous clefts, which cut up the country in every direction, and render observation as well as travel extremely difficult. The clefts carved by erosion vary from cracks measured by inches to cañons half a mile wide and hundreds of feet deep. They branch out in every direction, ramifying through the country after the manner of tree-roots in the soil, from each root a rootlet, from these other small fibres, until the system of passages develops into a labyrinth of far-reaching and intermingling lanes. Were the loëss throughout of the uniform structure seen in single clefts, such a region would be absolutely impassable, the vertical banks becoming often precipices of more than a thousand feet. The fact, however, that loëss exhibits all over a terrace formation renders its surface not only habitable, but highly convenient for agricultural purposes.

Different theories have been advanced in explana-

tion of this curious formation. Richtoven's theory
that it is a sub-aërial deposit is now most generally,
though not universally, adopted. It is enough to
say that the loëss gives to this part of the world
quite a unique appearance. Looking up from the
deep cut of a road below, you see nothing but walls
of loam, and tier after tier of loëss ridges. If you
ascend some lofty height, you will find a succession
of broader or narrower terraces, all of them carefully
cultivated with (in the season) green fields and waving
crops.

The extreme ease with which the loëss is cut
away tends at times seriously to embarrass traffic.
Dust made by the cart-wheels in the highway is
taken up by the high winds during the dry season
and blown over the surrounding lands, much after
the manner in which it was originally deposited here.
This action continuing over centuries, and assisted
by occasional deluges of rain, which find a ready
channel in the roads, has hollowed the country
routes into depressions of often fifty or a hundred
feet. This formation is very productive. The farmer
here has a harvest two and even three times a year
with constant tillage. There is no exhaustion of
the soil, and the only manure needed is a sprinkling
of its own loam obtained from the nearest bank, and
mingled with a little of that manure which is so
industriously gathered from the highways. From
a period of more than 2000 years before Christ the
province of Shansi has borne the name of the
Granary of the Empire,' while its yellow earth
(hwang-tu) is the origin of the imperial colour. The

peculiar character of the soil, however, is associated with one very serious drawback—a copious rainfall is more necessary here than elsewhere, and drought and famine are synonymous terms.

Before arriving at T'ai-yuen-fu, we stopped for a night at Shih-Tieh, a recently commenced station under the care of Mr. Morgan; it has a population of about 3500, and, being situated in the midst of a somewhat thickly peopled district, it does a considerable trade. Mr. Morgan came out from T'ai-yuen-fu to meet and entertain us, and we spent the evening in very pleasant intercourse with several intelligent and well-informed natives connected with the Christain community there.

CHAPTER VIII.

T'AI-YUEN-FU.

T'AI-YUEN-FU, the capital of this province, lies on the northern border of a large and fertile plain, about 3000 feet above the sea-level, and with an area of some 2000 square miles. It is difficult to get at the population of Chinese cities. Comparing it with others I have seen, I should estimate the population at about 60,000. The natives give a much higher figure, but Chinese statistics are proverbially un-reliable. T'ai-yuen-fu is the centre of the Baptist Mission work in Shansi, and though we approached the city in a driving snowstorm, the missionaries and a number of native Christians, according to Chinese custom, came forth to meet us and bid us welcome.

On Sunday we had the opportunity of seeing something of both the Baptist and China Inland Missions. As the China Inland Mission native service is held an hour earlier than our own, we were able to spend a little time with them. Afterwards, at our own service, we had a very enjoyable time, Dr. Glover and myself addressing the natives, who seemed very pleased to see and hear us. In the evening we had an English service, at which the resident families of both missions were present, with two or three missionaries who were passing through the city. Our time in T'ai-yuen-fu was largely taken up with the conferences which we held with our brethren about mission work. They would have been glad if our visit had fallen at some other time than the Chinese New Year. It is so complete and universal a holiday that it is difficult to get people together, and in consequence the congregations have been smaller than they would have been at any other season. We, however, had the opportunity of witnessing the new year's festivities in this large city; and what we saw here may be regarded as fairly representing what takes place on a larger or smaller scale in every part of this vast empire.

The Chinese New Year is a movable festival, and it fell in 1891 on February 9, according to our calendar. The Chinese divide their year into twelve lunar months, with an additional month introduced as required, two of these intercalary months coming in, I believe, within every period of five years. But while the year is divided into lunar months, the commencement of the year is determined by the sun, the year dating from the first new moon after the sun enters Aquarius. New Year's Day may, therefore, fall on any day between January 21 and February 19. The great holiday extends from the first to the fifteenth day of their first month. Indeed, all public business is at a standstill till the twentieth of the month, in token of which fact all official seals and documents are locked up during the whole of this time. On the morning of the twentieth these seals are brought out again with great ceremony, though the actual business of the new year does not commence till the next day. To a great extent there is during this holiday-time the cessation of private as well as public business, shops and warehouses being generally, and for some days, universally closed. After the first few days, however, the cessation of business is not so complete as I was led to expect, small and impecunious traders being obliged to yield to the pressure of circumstances, and open their shops one after another, while wealthier shopkeepers show their independence by keeping their establishments closed for a longer time. Still, with all these variations, it is a longer and more complete holiday season than can be found in any other nation. The New Year's Day itself is the great day, and its advent is announced by a demonstrative and noisy celebration throughout the night preceding. There is an almost constant discharge of squibs and crackers, and the streets are the next morning almost covered with the cases of these exploded fireworks, and for several days these crackers are going off, though not in equal numbers. It is a comical sight to see a middle-aged or elderly Chinaman deliberately put down a large cracker on the road, ignite it with his incense stick, and, with solemn and unmoved face, watch the explosions that ensue, and then retire to his house like a man who feels that he has adequately discharged one of the most important duties of life.

The last month of the old year is largely taken up with preparations for the new year. In almost every house in China such work of preparation is going forward. The not unnecessary work of house-cleaning is at last attended to—most houses are swept and garnished. The filthy accumulations of eleven months are in some way or other disposed of—got out of sight in this last month of the year. The people re-paper the windows, and put up new paper mottoes on doors, doorposts, and lintels. Costly garments, only used on important occasions, are got out in readiness for the new year, and it is the great time when all who can afford to do so provide themselves with new clothing. Those who cannot afford to buy, borrow smart-looking dresses, with which they make an imposing appearance during the holiday.

It is a busy season with all tradesmen ; the accounts of the year have to be made up before its close, all outstanding liabilities must be met, and all outstanding debts, if possible, must be got in ; for if not paid by the new year there will be but little chance of getting them in before the next new year. The rule in China is that all debts must be paid before the end of the year, and a man is said to 'lose face,' *i.e.* character or reputation, if he does not square up with his creditors by that time; but in China, as elsewhere, there are many people who have not much reputation to lose in that particular, and those tradesmen and others to whom accounts are owing have a busy time of it for a week or two before New Year's Day, and especially the last few days of the year, hunting up defaulters.

The twenty-third day of the last moon is one of special significance in every Chinese home. The kitchen-god then returns to the spirit-world, to give his account of the doings and misdoings of the household over which he has presided. This god is usually represented by a sheet of thin paper with two important and several subordinate personages rudely depicted on it. This picture is hung up over the cooking-stove, and from that position he keeps the proceedings of the household under observation, sending brief monthly reports to his superior; but at the close of the year he departs to render in person a more minute account of all that has transpired during the year, and, with the hope of propitiating him, offerings of sweetmeats and wine are set before him. The sweetmeats are smeared over his lips, so that they may impede utterance, and he is steeped in wine, so that, being intoxicated, he may fail to remember what he intended to say, or give such an incoherent account of what he has seen, that little attention will be paid to it. Having taken these precautions, the paper is burned, and the kitchen-god is supposed to enter the spirit-world with his annual report.

Immediately before the new year great labour is expended in the preparation of food, and especially in the manufacture in immense quantities of the famous pien-shehs, of which every family partakes at the New Year's morning meal. These pien-shehs are small boiled dumplings, about the size of a walnut, or rather larger, filled with finely chopped meat and vegetables. Pieces of money are placed in several of these, and whoever obtains one of these is supposed to have a prosperous future before him.

One of the things to be attended to on New Year's Day is worship before the ancestral tablets, after which the children of the household pay homage to their parents. There is also the formal reception of the kitchen-god, who is set up in his place, and is supposed to have come down from heaven, but who was really purchased for a few cash a day or two before. Another ceremony of New Year's Day, practised throughout China, is the worship of the emperor. A gentleman who was present gave me the following account of what took place in the emperor's temple, as it is called, in T'ai-yuen-fu. The provincial governor and all the subordinate officials assembled there, and before a throne made in imitation of the dragon throne, and on which is a tablet bearing the inscription, ' May the emperor reign ten thousand years and ten times ten thousand years,' they prostrated themselves nine times. They then retired to an outer court, where tea was served, and the provincial governor having been saluted by all subordinates, and New

Year's congratulations and good wishes exchanged, there was a further adjournment to the Temple of Confucius, and homage similar to that rendered to the emperor paid at the altar of China's great sage. There is a saying here, ' Confucius is greater than the emperor,' for while all worship the emperor, the emperor himself worships Confucius. Had I known of the ceremony in time, I would have been present, as the temple referred to is quite near the house where I was then staying.

The early days of the new year are largely devoted to the exchange of complimentary calls. All callers are not received ; if you do not wish to see any one you send out the message, ' I dare not presume to detain you,' and the caller leaves his card, which is understood as conveying to you the compliments of the season, and passes on to the house of another friend or acquaintance to go through the same cere-mony. Every one in China is supposed to add another year to his age on New Year's Day. Thus, a child born on the last day of the old year will be spoken of on New Year's morning as two years old, *i.e.* the child is in its second year.

On the fourth day of the Chinese new year we had to start for Hsin-chow, the centre of one of the most important branches of the Shansi Mission, a journey occupying nearly two days. We had the idea before coming to China that travelling for the first ten days of the new year would be difficult, if not impossible. It is not the time one would choose for travelling, but we experienced no difficulty or inconvenience.

We reached Hsin-chow after a journey which would

have been pleasant but for the dust with which at times we were almost smothered. I was surprised at seeing so large an amount of heavy traffic on the road thus early in the new year. In this part of China, goods are carried almost exclusively by heavy freight carts, the usual two-wheeled carts, upon which immense loads are packed. These are drawn by one mule in the shafts, and two or three loosely harnessed in front. The leading animals are attached by strong rope traces, not to the shafts, but to the axletree of the cart.

We were greatly interested in what we saw of the mission work in Hsin-chow. We spent several hours after our arrival in having interviews with the natives, who came in in small parties of four or five at a time, for all were anxious to see and have a chat with the Lao-mou-shihs, who had come so many thousand li to visit them. One of their number, as representing the rest, intimated that they would have liked to provide food for us, but the shops being closed they could not do so. They, however, begged our acceptance of two boxes of confectionery. On the Sunday morning we had a native service, at which about a hundred were present, and in the afternoon a communion service. On Monday morning we set off again to visit an out-station—Chi-tsuen—about half a day's journey from Hsin-chow. On our way we stopped by invitation at the house of a well-to-do Chinese family, to a member of which Mr. Dixon, one of the Baptist missionaries, rendered an important surgical service some time ago, by which he has endeared himself to the whole household. They seemed delighted to see us, and to have the opportunity of entertaining us. A bountiful repast was set before us, and at another table and in another room food was provided for our servants and muleteers. You would have been amused to see us squatting on the k'ang, our food on a k'ang table, and we performing with our chopsticks in the presence of a large number of onlookers who knew so much better how to use them than ourselves. We were conducted over the large establishment, and were glad of the opportunity of seeing the domestic arrangements of a well-appointed Chinese house.

Near this village, which is situated at the foot of the mountains which form the north-west boundary of the Hsin-chow plain, there are two very noticeable conical hills, which from their shapes and relative positions have gained for themselves the name of the Breasts of Hsin-chow; the summit of each hill is crowned with a temple, while near the base of one there rise some springs of tepid water, with which another temple is associated. There is an interesting work carried on in the little market town of Chi-tsuen. We had in the evening a well-attended service, though here, as elsewhere, several who are usually present at the services were away, owing to the New Year's holiday. The next day we returned to Hsin-chow, and then, after a short rest, to T'ai-yuen-fu.

From T'ai-yuen-fu I went over to one of the out-stations, a small market town known by the name of Hsiao-tien-tzu. This meant starting early, and spending seven hours in a Chinese cart. In every village through which we passed we saw much to remind us that the New Year's holiday was not over, and that the Feast of Lanterns, which practically brings that holiday to a close, was near at hand. As I drew nearer to the town I saw on the top of a disused tower a number of men, and wondered what they were doing there. I presently learned that they were representatives of the native Christians, who had been for some time on the watch for our approach, so that, seeing us at a distance, they might be prepared to go forth to meet and welcome us. We had a goodly gathering at the service ; the natives were delighted to see us, expressed their wonder that men so old should have come so far, and wished us to convey their greetings to their Christian brethren in England. After partaking of a meal of native food, we returned to the city, tired, but delighted with what we had seen and heard. Altogether we had a very pleasant time with the Chinese Christians.

One thing that strikes a stranger travelling in China is the number of mottoes, usually written or printed on red paper, pasted up on walls, doors, shop-fronts, and even on carts and wheel-barrows. At the new year old ones are removed, and new ones put up. From time to time I asked my travelling companion to translate a few of these inscriptions. Two or three may be taken as a sample: 'Agriculture is the fountain from which gold flows,' over a shop for sale of agricultural implements. 'The Hall of life's renewal,' over native opium refuge. 'The Spring of everlasting righteousness,' the motto over a shop of a general dealer, where for any article you would at first be asked at least double the amount which the tradesman expected ultimately to receive. On another shop door-post we read, 'A spice of honesty makes life peaceful as a river.' On another shop door, 'The budding promises of wealth are more numerous than the blossoms of spring.' A wayside inn was designated, ' The inn of obedience and good instruction.' Over the door of a private house we read, 'May the dwellers in this house have long life, great prosperity, and many male children.' On another, 'One door and five blessednesses,' *i.e.* may the five Chinese beatitudes pass in through that one doorway. One of the most curious of these mottoes was over the door of an undertaker : ' To die is but to go home.' Many of these inscriptions are very striking and beautiful ; but if any one wishes to be convinced of the powerlessness of mere moral sentiment to elevate and regenerate society, let him go to China.

The Chinese Feast of Lanterns is announced by a more profuse discharge of squibs and crackers than occurs the night before New Year's Day. My bedroom being separated from the street by only a wall, I was kept awake by the almost continual discharge of these crackers, some of them going off with a very violent explosion. The day falls on the fifteenth of the first moon. There is a very remarkable tradition prevailing in Shansi, but I could not ascertain if it were only a local tradition. In the ages long gone by, a god looked down upon the world, and saw that it was wholly given up to wickedness, and determined to destroy it by fire, fixing the fifteenth day of the first moon for the fulfilment of his purpose. Some in his court, however, sent a messenger secretly to declare to the world what their lord was about to do, and to advise that on the evening of that day one or more lights should be placed in the doorway of every building, and fires kindled before the houses, so that the god on his approach, seeing the unusual glare, might suppose that his purpose was already accomplished, and go back quietly to his abode. The advice was acted upon, and so the world was saved, and from that time to this the Feast of Lanterns has been observed in commemoration of this great deliverance.

It is a great day throughout China, and is certainly the most brilliant festival of the year. For days before extensive decorations, chiefly of coloured paper, are put in their proper places, and not only does the great city, but every miserable collection of mud huts, and indeed every solitary dwelling, join in the celebrations. One of the earliest ceremonies of the day is the worship of Confucius by the Fu-tai (provincial governor) and all subordinate officials ; a ceremony similar in character to that already referred to as performed on the first day of the month. During the day, processions, larger or smaller, composed of men and boys fantastically dressed, are moving about the streets of the city, some of them reminding me of those which are still seen in our streets on Guy Fawke's Day, and which some of us remember to have seen in earlier days on the 1st of May in the procession of chimney-sweeps. These, however, are more elaborate affairs, and are regarded with the utmost seriousness by on-lookers, as constituting important and significant parts of a great national celebration. These, to me, unmeaning processions of mummers represented, I was told, scenes in well-known historical plays.

All that occurs during the day, however, is only intended to lead up to and prepare the way for the festivities of the evening. That we might with the least inconvenience witness the display, we engaged carts, and were driven through the more important streets of the city ; had we wished to do so, we could scarcely have made our way on foot, as there had been a thaw during the day, and the roadway, which occupies nearly the entire width of a Chinese street, was covered to a depth of three or four inches with liquid filth, and besides that it would have been a matter of great difficulty for a party of foreigners to elbow their way through a Chinese street on such an occasion. As it was, our white faces and white hair secured a great deal of attention, and elicited many expressions of good-humoured astonishment. Every house was more or less effectively illuminated with lanterns of various sizes and shapes—round, square, oblong—while some are fashioned to grotesquely represent different animals, real and imaginary ; some lanterns were very ingeniously constructed with moving figures representing fishes swimming or a procession of camels, the movement being secured by the action of the heated air. The lanterns were chiefly covered with paper of various colours, the prevailing colour being red, the symbol of joy and festivity.

The grandest display was in the principal business street, a long, straight, narrow street in which every shop on either side was adorned with a large number of paper lanterns ; and besides, these many shops had ingeniously constructed transparencies showing either appropriate mottoes or historical scenes. The

I

long line of street thus illuminated presented a very brilliant appearance. In addition to these house-illuminations there were, every few yards, large blazing bonfires, which were carefully fed with wood and coal, and displays of fireworks let off in the middle of the streets, some of which were very effective, while squibs and crackers were being fired in every direction. The narrow footways were crowded with people, who seemed to have two objects in view—the one to see all there was to be seen, the other to avoid being pushed off into the indescribable filth of the roadway. The roadway itself was almost as much crowded with carts, conveying sightseers like ourselves, as the sideways were with foot-passengers. I admired very much the unmoved equanimity of the mules. My mule would stand perfectly un-disturbed with his nose only a few yards from a fountain of fire rising up in front of him, and crackers exploding on every side. The illumination began as soon as it was dark, and was all over by nine o'clock.

While in T'ai-yuen-fu I paid a visit to a Taouist temple. I went there with the expectation of seeing a performance corresponding in character with the *planchette* performance of modern spiritualists. It is effected by means of an iron rod or pencil suspended from the roof of the temple over a large plate of sand, upon the smooth surface of which it inscribes what are accepted as oracular responses coming through that medium from the presiding deity. On reaching the temple, we found that the practice had been dis-continued. So-called oracular responses are, how-ever, still vouchsafed. These are distributed into several different classes—remedies for diseases, directions for business, family matters, etc.—and there are as many cylindrical vases, made of sections of bamboo, about ten inches in height, containing thirty or forty slips of wood separately numbered. Corresponding with these, in their different classes, are the responses, printed on yellow paper, and hung in small bundles on the walls of the temple. What I saw while in the temple will afford some idea of the way in which the responses are obtained. Two respectable women arrived in a cart about the same time as ourselves, apparently mother and daughter. They first of all presented their offering, burned their bundles of incense-sticks, and prostrated themselves, bowing with their heads to the ground nine times ; the younger woman then received from the priest one of the vases, and, kneeling down, she shook it till one of the sticks fell to the ground ; the priest then picked it up and gave it to the boy in attendance, who removed from the wall a paper with the number corresponding with that on the stick. The young woman then went through the same ceremony for her companion, who was apparently too old to perform it for herself, and the two went away seeming quite satisfied with the result of their visit. I may add that the ceremony described commences with the sounding of a gong, to call the attention of the god to those who are waiting at his shrine. Outside the temple we met a man who was going away with one of these yellow pieces of paper. He told us that he had been ill for some time, that the native doctors had failed to cure him, and that he had obtained now a recipe from the gods, which he should take to a chemist's and have made up. The poor fellow looked as though he needed effective treatment.

The day after the Feast of Lanterns we had a heavy fall of snow, which continued the next day, so that the evening before the day fixed for our departure our friends questioned if we should be wise to start on our mountain journey. The head muleteer, predicting slow progress, expressed his willingness to go if we wished ; and near the appointed time we started on our fortnight's journey to Peking, Mr. Morgan accompanying us. When we got among the mountains, our progress was slower than it would have been without snow, but we enjoyed our journey notwithstanding. The broken masses of limestone, granite, and sandstone, with the equally broken but more regularly interrupted loëss formation, with its terraces and precipices clothed or flecked with snow, presented a succession of pictures the beauty of which amply compensated us for any little delay or inconvenience occasioned by the snowstorm. Had the snow caused us much greater inconvenience, we should have welcomed it, as conferring a great boon upon many millions of anxious people. With scarcely any snow in the earlier winter, there would have been an almost utter failure of the wheat harvest in May, had not this snow come ; as it was, it came just in time.

The road from T'ai-yuen-fu to Hwai-lu, after the first stage, is a wild mountain-pass, and the track—you can scarcely call it a road—often runs along the edge of a precipice, the loëss cliffs rising to some height above you on one side, and falling several hundred feet on the other. The mules, guided only

by their own sweet will and the voice of the driver,
who walks by their side, have a way of taking the
more perilous side of the road, as it appears to the
passenger. In these circumstances you are powerless.
A foreigner can by no words at his command convey
his wishes to a Chinese mule, and he experiences
almost as much difficulty in dealing with a Chinese
muleteer. I only once ventured on a remonstrance,
and then without satisfactory result. At a sharp
bend in the road (not on this journey) my mules
came to stand at the tail end of a long line of carts
which preceded us, hindered by some block in the
road further on. Looking out, I found my conveyance, an erh-ma-jü, a sedan chair suspended
between poles, like the mule litter, was projecting
an inch or two over a precipice one hundred and fifty
or two hundred feet in depth. Had this been the
only standing ground, complaint would have been
unreasonable ; but in the curve on the off side the
mules might have taken up their position, leaving a
yard and a half of road between them and the abyss.
I tried to persuade the muleteer to lead them into
that place of safety, pointing to the precipice and
the unoccupied roadway and the mules, employing
gesticulations which occurred to me as appropriate
and suggestive, but all to no purpose. There the
good fellow stood, showing his white teeth, and
smiling all over his face, and protesting, I have no
doubt, his willingness, and even anxiety, to do whatever I wished ; but the one particular thing which I
did wish I utterly failed to make him understand.

On our way to Hwai-lu we met no fewer than

thirteen coffins slung between poles, on the same principle as the mule litters. These were being conveyed to ancestral burial-places in Shansi or other provinces beyond the hills. On each of these coffins, with three exceptions, I noticed a small bamboo cage, containing a white cock. This cock, I have been told, represents one of the three spirits which the departed was supposed to possess, and was to render service by driving away evil spirits, and, by crowing, to let the dead man's spirit know when they start, that it may not be left behind. The cock is, I believe, in some instances sacrificed at the grave-side. These customs have apparently different interpretations in different districts.

Shansi is one of the great opium-consuming and opium-producing provinces, and the streets of T'ai-yuen-fu show many cadaverous and emaciated faces belonging to opium-smokers. On the other hand, some who have taken opium for years show the effects of it very slightly in their faces. It is difficult to ascertain what proportion of the population of Shansi indulge in this habit. A very intelligent native told me that he thought there would be six or seven opium-smokers out of ten men in the city, while in the country the proportion would not be more than three to ten. He also said that when he was a boy—he was nearly seventy years of age—opium was consumed, but that the habit of using it was not a common one, and an opium-smoker was pointed at and talked of as quite an exceptional character. The practice, he told us, had grown up chiefly during the last thirty years. Native-grown opium is almost exclusively used in

Shansi. Being much cheaper than foreign, it is also less potent, and therefore, we may hope, less harmful. The practice—which, I fear, is on the increase— every one admits to be most harmful; and it so weakens the moral nature and will power that to break away from the habit is most difficult. Many say that scarcely any lasting cures are effected, save where powerful religious motives are brought into operation. There is considerable diversity of opinion as to the value of opium refuges. I should think, from all I have heard, that they render valuable service where they are under skilled and responsible management. In Chih-li and Shantung opium is smoked, but to a much smaller extent than in Shansi. As a set-off to opium-smoking, there is no visible drunkenness in the interior of China; in the parts, at least, I have visited I have not seen a drunken man. I have scarcely seen a Chinaman taking anything stronger than the weakest of weak tea or hot water. The Chinese never think of drinking cold water; and, seeing the amount of filth existing in immediate proximity to the wells from which their water is ordinarily taken, it is a very fortunate thing that the drinking water in China is almost invariably boiled before it is consumed.

The journey from T'ai-yuen-fu to Peking was long and interesting. We left the mountains at Hwai-lu, but travelled within sight of them during the greater part of the journey, so that when we grew weary with the monotony of the plain we could get immediate refreshment by looking to the rugged outlines stand-ing out distinctly from the unclouded sky on the

western boundary; in many places we could discern
the snowy sides and summits of a loftier and remoter
range.   All through the journey we had evidence of
the return of spring, and could watch the different
agricultural processes with which Chinese farmers and
labourers were everywhere busy.

The implements of husbandry are of the most
simple and primitive kind, and yet seem well
adapted to the light and easily worked soil of the
district.   The plough is of exceedingly light construction—a man could carry one home on his shoulder.
The harrow is a small wooden frame with iron teeth,
so light that it would of itself scarcely scratch the
soil, but the Chinaman saves himself the labour of
walking, and gives the teeth of the harrow the necessary penetrating power by balancing himself on the
frame as it is dragged across the field.   It may interest
agricultural readers to know that the Chinese have a
winnowing machine working with a fan, in principle
precisely like that with which East Anglian farmers
are familiar—we probably borrowed the idea from the
Celestials.   These machines, however, are only used
by the better-to-do farmers ; the earliest and simplest
method is still commonly employed.   The threshed
grain is tossed in the air, and the wind drives away
‘ the chaff of the summer threshing-floor.’

We spent a part of Saturday and a very pleasant
Sunday at Pao-ting-fu (pronounced Bodingfoo), a
large and important city, the capital of the province
of Chih-li.   It is a very important business centre,
situated at the intersection of several of the great
roads of China, and, when the river is not frozen up,

having water communication with Tien-tsin and the
coast. During our stay we were the guests of Dr.
and Mrs. Merritt, of the American Board of Missions.
The work at this station is of a very encouraging
kind. On the Sunday I spoke to the natives in the
morning, and my colleague addressed them in the
afternoon. There were large and apparently interested
congregations. It is impossible to over-estimate the
importance of these centres of Christian influence
and of a higher civilization, which are multiplying all
over China. Here, as in many otγer places, we were
made to feel how important a part medical missions
are playing in the evangelization of this great empire.

After leaving Pao-ting-fu we passed through several
places of importance, among which we may mention
Chow-chow, a busy place, with two fine pagodas, near
which there is a long stone bridge adorned with lions
and elephants, while further on we came to the still
finer bridge of Loo-Kow-Chian, which is celebrated
for the two hundred and eighty stone lions which
crown the parapets, and the stone elephants which
keep guard at either end. At the time of our visit
there was but little water in the river which the
bridge spans, but we were told that in the rainy
season it swells into a mighty stream. We were
interested in noticing at this bridge the most serious
attempt at substantial repairs that we had anywhere
met with. We then crossed several miles of country
where everything bore witness to the desolating
force of those floods which so often lay waste the
low-lying districts in the neighbourhood of Chinese
rivers. And then we came to an imposing-looking

Pailow, which seemed intended to form the commencement of the imperial stone road which for about seven
miles constitutes the approach to the city of Peking—
a road which has been so worn by the traffic of many
generations that its surface has become distressingly
unequal ; and as all the traffic to and from the west
and south-west passes over this road, it was, when
we saw it, more crowded with passengers and trains
of animals laden with merchandise than any road on
which we have travelled in China.

This once magnificent road is, like all the other
public works of this great empire, falling into a state
of almost hopeless dilapidation and decay. No
private person has a right to repair an imperial road,
and there is no public authority which seems to take
public convenience into account. When complaining
of inn accommodation in Shantung and Shansi, we
were told that we should find better accommodation
on the road to Peking. The difference, however,
between the best and the worst is not very considerable. And on this high-road to Peking we experienced an annoyance which we only encountered
once in all our previous travels, and that is, the
invasion of the innyards by singing girls of questionable character, who force their way into the rooms
of the guests if the doors are left open or unbarred,
and who are not easily got rid of if they once enter.
Night after night we were disturbed by their not very
melodious songs and the twanging of their guitar
accompaniment. We complained to the landlords
of these inns, but, while they made us fair promises
that we should not be annoyed, we experienced no
abatement of the nuisance.

CHAPTER IX.

PEKING.

Approach to the city—Multitude of camels—Busy spectacle—Description of the city—Chinese city—Tartar city—' Carnation prohibited city '—The ' unspeakably dirty city '—The ' land-ship of mercy ' —Funeral processions—The Altar of Heaven—The Altar of Earth — The astronomical observatory — Examination Hall — Lama monastery—Great Bell Temple—Imperial college—Missionary and philanthropic work—Dr. Blodget and the American Board— Methodist Episcopal Mission — London Missionary Society— American Presbyterian Mission—Society for the Propagation of the Gospel—Roman Catholic Missions—Portuguese cemetery.

ON the fifteenth day after leaving T'ai-yuen-fu we drew near Peking. Our progress during the last few miles was very slow, owing to the immense amount of traffic on the road ; for miles it swarmed with camels. In about three hours I counted 2113. This does not represent the entire number we passed, for in many places they were so numerous that it was quite impossible to enumerate them. Many of these at the close of the winter season were going back light to Mongolia, Thibet, and elsewhere, and looked as though they needed to be fed up in prospect of another winter's work. The road by which we entered Peking presented one of the busiest spectacles I ever witnessed. It is of great breadth, and lined with shops on either side ; in the centre is a raised causeway—the road proper ; immediately in front of the shops on either side is a small space reserved for foot-passengers, while the spaces between the road and foot-ways, averaging not less than fifty feet on either side, are occupied with the stalls of traders, or more frequently the goods offered for sale are spread out on the ground. Almost every inch of unoccupied ground was taken up with sellers and buyers, or interested spectators. Through the densely crowded streets we slowly, very slowly, passed—I in my erh-ma-jü (a kind of conveyance not often seen in Peking), and we excited a great deal of interest, and many remarks—whether complimentary or otherwise my knowledge of Chinese does not enable me to say.

Peking (*i.e.* the northern capital, as Nanking is the southern capital) is situated on a sandy plain about twelve miles south-west of the Peiho. Though distinguished by the decay and dilapidation everywhere visible in China, there are traces and remains of former magnificence which cannot fail to interest and impress every visitor. It is a large city— the area within the walls is nearly twenty-six square miles ; the suburbs are small and unimportant. The population is estimated at about 1,000,000, made up of Mongols, Manchus, and Chinese, the Chinese probably far outnumbering all the others. In former times there is reason for believing that the population was much greater than it is at present. The Chinese regard Peking as one of their ancient cities, but it was not made the capital of the whole empire till Kublai established his court here in 1264. It was then called, in Chinese, Ta-tu, 'the great capital,' and in Mongol, Khanbalih, 'City of the Khan.' It might well be called the great capital, not only because of its extent, but because it was the metropolis of one of the largest empires ever ruled over by a single man. On the overthrow of the Mongol dynasty, Nanking was made the capital city, and remained so until Yunglo established his court in Kublai in 1409, calling it Peking, 'The Northern Capital,' and it has continued to be the capital city of the empire from that time to the present.

Peking consists of two cities, known by the Chinese as Inner and Outer, but by foreigners spoken of as Tartar and Chinese cities. These are only divided by a wall, pierced by three gates, and they form in reality only one city. The southern (or Chinese) city is a parallelogram, about five miles long by two broad ; the wall which encloses it is twenty-two feet high and fifteen feet broad at the top, and a little over nine miles in length, the northern boundary of the Chinese city being formed by the southern wall of the Tartar city. The Tartar or (Manchu) city is enclosed by the finest wall surrounding any existing city. It is forty-five and a half feet high, and forty-seven and a quarter feet broad at the top. The surface is paved with large brick flags, and protected by a battlemented parapet on each side. Buttresses (or towers) occur every sixty yards, each projecting fifty feet, and every sixth one being twice the size of the others. The wall is pierced by nine gates—three on the south side and two on each of the remaining sides. Each gateway is surrounded by a large semicircular wall or *enceinte*, and is surmounted by a lofty tower over a hundred feet in height, similar towers standing at each of the four corners of the city. As no buildings in the city are lofty, the only thing that breaks the monotonous level is the enclosing wall with its bastions and towers.

The southern city is chiefly occupied by Chinese. It is densely populated, and most of the business of Peking (wholesale and retail) is done here. The banks and more important mercantile houses are crowded together near the central gate (or Chien-Men), as the Chinese call it; the streets are lined with shops, in which, if you look for it, almost everything you want can be obtained. Different streets, or sections of streets, seem to be devoted to special lines of business. Some of the shops are very elaborately decorated with wood carving and gilding, but as a rule they have a dismal, uninviting appearance. There is no window display such as Englishmen are accustomed to. All the shops open up to the street. The goods are stored away on shelves, and in drawers or boxes in the rear. The salesmen stand on the inside of the counter; the purchasers stand (or sit) on the outside, everything being open to the observation and criticisms of the crowd that speedily gathers. A foreigner is often surprised at the large collection of costly goods to be found in a shop that makes no display whatever. In the broad spaces on either side of the central roadway are booths and stalls for the sale of different kinds of merchandise, and there are many itinerant salesmen who have not a stall to cover their goods. A large trade is done in the sale of cooked food of all descriptions, and by means of a variety of ingenious contrivances this cooking is done in the open streets. Another feature of Peking is the way in which tradesmen on either side of the street take possession of large spaces in front of their own places of business—timber, stone, and bricks being piled up in large quantities. One of these streets, seen in the busiest part of the day, is a sight to be remembered. Besides the local traders, there is an immense number of pedlars and itinerant salesmen— cooks who carry their establishments with them, barbers who are shaving heads and plaiting pigtails by the wayside, sellers of fruit and flowers and vegetables, tapes, ribbons, old shoes, and older clothes, with all that they contain—each wandering trades-man proclaiming his existence by means of his own distinctive rattle or gong. In the vacant spaces that are left, one sees showmen, acrobats, conjurers, story-tellers, with a larger or smaller crowd around them ; while in every place there are the beggars, who con-stitute a distinct profession, with parti-coloured rags which scarcely cover their nakedness, and which are artistically arranged to display to the fullest extent their dirt, disease, or deformity. These beggars ply their 'calling' with an amount of audacity and pertinacity which makes them the plague of Peking. While the sideways are thus thronged, the central roadway is crowded with mules, donkeys, camels, and carts, of which we were told there are probably nearly 20,000 plying for hire in Peking.

The Tartar city is a much larger place. It consists of three nearly concentric squares or parallelograms. The external one is the Tartar city ; then comes the Imperial city, and within that the ' Carnation Prohibited City ' or ' Forbidden City.' The Tartar city—the abode of the Manchus—may be regarded as a sort of armed encampment, held by the descendants of the great Manchu army that conquered China and took Peking in 1644. They are divided into eight banners or regiments ; all the male Manchus receive a monthly allowance, the cost to the Government being, it is said, £160,000 per month. They form an army reserve, and are liable to be called out at any time. The Manchu women do not cripple their feet ; and they enjoy much more liberty than the Chinese women. Within the Tartar city is the second enclosure, which is known as the Hwang Chang, or Imperial City, forming an oblong rectangle ; the surrounding wall measures about six miles, having a gate on each side. Within this, again, is another walled enclosure, its circuit being two and a quarter miles. This contains the palace of the emperor, with its surrounding buildings. It is called T'zi-Ku-Chang, or ' Carnation Prohibited City.' Of this nothing can be seen but the yellow-tiled roofs of the imperial residence. The pleasure-grounds of the emperor, which are about a mile and a half in circumference, are surrounded—like nearly everything else in China—with a wall, but the picturesque hill which forms part of it can be seen. It is about a hundred feet in height, well covered with trees, and on each of its five peaks is a Buddhist temple. It is an artificial hill, raised, it is supposed, of earth dug out of the neighbouring lakes. It is known as the Coal Hill, because, tradition says, a large quantity of coal is stored away in it, to provide against a possible winter siege. It was on this hill that the last emperor of the Ming dynasty hanged himself just before the Manchus took Peking. On the west side of the palace and Prospect Hill are the imperial pleasure lakes, spanned by a splendid marble bridge six hundred and sixty feet long. Of this lake we only got a glimpse through an open gateway.

In Peking a very large number of important officials dwell. You often meet them in their yellow, green, or red sedan chairs, with a large number of attendants ; there must be a large number of fine residences, but the visitor sees nothing of them but the decorated roofs and enclosing walls. In the residential parts of the city you may go for miles through streets and narrow lanes with nothing but blank walls on either side, broken by occasional doorways. No Chinese house has windows opening out on the street or road. This gives to Peking, when you are out of its great business thoroughfares, that dreary, monotonous appearance which is characteristic of all Chinese cities. From the top of the outer wall, the city appears to the greatest advantage. You see the yellow roofs of the imperial palace, the green roofs of princes and high officials, the loftier elevations of towers and temples, with an immense number of finely grown trees, with which the gardens and courtyards are planted, altogether forming a very pleasant picture ; and if this were the only view

K

obtainable, you would question if Peking deserved to be spoken of as the 'unspeakably dirty city.' After closer inspection, however, you are little inclined to rob it of this unenviable distinction. The streets, except at the bridges and gateways, are not paved, but are merely hard-trodden earth, covered with a thick layer of dust in dry weather and a thick layer of mud in wet weather; all the refuse of the neighbouring houses is thrown into the roadway, while on either side of the raised cart-track in the centre of the street are trenches—so many cesspools, in which liquid abominations are left to seethe and fester. The more important thoroughfares are regularly watered, the sewage from adjacent cesspools being lifted up in buckets and distributed over the dusty road by the city police, who are about as disreputable-looking a set of men as ever held office in an imperial city. This street-watering is attended to every afternoon between four and six o'clock, and the foreigner who passes through the streets at this time wishes he were as destitute of the sense of smell as the Chinese appear to be. The habits of the common people are as disgusting as the sanitary provisions are defective. Probably in no other civilized city in the world are the common decencies of life so unblushingly disregarded.

I was not out early enough to see it, but I was told that every morning a buffalo-cart, called the Lu-ti-tsz-hang (or 'land-ship of mercy'), goes through each ward of the city, collecting the bodies of children that have died since it made its previous round; these, wrapped in straw or matting, or placed in

rough wooden boxes, are carried forth and deposited
in a pit prepared for the purpose, without ceremony
or service. Funerals are the most costly things in
which the Chinese indulge. We saw, while at
Peking, two funeral processions of persons in good
position, but not of distinguished rank ; in each case
a large number of men and boys, the ragamuffins of
the city, were employed carrying the hearse—or,
rather, a huge and highly decorated covered bier—
tablets, umbrellas, and a great variety of things, the
significance of which I did not understand. The
sedan chairs in which the deceased had ridden,
the horses which had carried him, and even (on a
tray) the opium pipe which he had smoked—all had
place in the procession ; the undertaker provides
everything, even the persons who attend the funeral.
Each of those processions we saw was more than
half a mile in length. The funerals of high officials
are very imposing, and the processions so long that
they take two or three hours to pass a given point.
The persons employed by undertakers to carry the
different symbols are a very miscellaneous lot, not by
any means equal in appearance to the men and boys
used to carry sandwich boards in England, their only
personal distinction being a small tuft of red feathers,
which for the occasion they stick in their ragged and
greasy caps.

So far as we could spare time for that purpose, we
saw the principal objects of interest in Peking ; the
city itself we saw in visiting the different missions.
Perhaps the most interesting sight in the city is the
Tien-Tan—the Altar of Heaven. The enclosure con-

taining this is situated just within the south wall of the Chinese city. No one is admitted within the enclosure, but a friend assured us that we could get a good view of the altar from the south wall. To reach its summit was not perfectly easy. A silver key opened several gates, and we at last found ourselves at the foot of the double ascent to the top of the wall, but we also found the approaches to these had been carefully blocked with stones and bricks. We managed, by the removal of some at the top, to scale those that remained, and we at last found ourselves at the spot which we desired to reach, from which an excellent view of the altar, with its surrounding buildings and enclosures, is obtained. The south altar (the most important of Chinese religious edifices) consists of three circular terraces of white marble ; the lowest one is two hundred and ten feet in diameter, the next a hundred and fifty feet, the top one ninety feet, each being surrounded with a richly carved balustrade. The surface of the altar is paved with white marble. It is upon the central round stone that the emperor kneels when he worships at the winter solstice. About a hundred feet to the south-east of the altar is the great furnace, faced with green porcelain, and approached on three of its sides by porcelain steps. In this furnace is consumed, at the yearly ceremony, a bullock, whole and without blemish. Separated from the Altar of Heaven by a low wall was a smaller though more conspicuous building, called the Altar of Prayer for grain. It is somewhat similar to the south altar, but upon its upper terrace there formerly rose

a magnificent triple-roofed edifice, known by foreigners
as the Temple of Heaven. This was roofed with
blue tiles and surmounted with a golden ball. This
fine structure was struck by lightning a year and a
half ago, and utterly consumed. Outside the Tartar
city, on the north side, is the Altar of Earth, where
the emperor worships at the summer solstice. We
obtained a view of this from the northern wall. In
the eastern suburb there is an altar to the sun, while
on the west side is an altar to the moon. All these
altars are placed within large walled enclosures.

One day we paid a visit to the astronomical
observatory, which is built against and rises a few
feet above the south-east wall of the Tartar city. It
is the oldest observatory in the world ; it was founded
by Kublai, about the year 1279. The older instruments have been removed from the wall, and are
placed below in the front court. They are very fine
specimens of bronze casting, and represent the most
advanced astronomical knowledge of the period. On
the observatory itself are the instruments which were
made under the direction of Verbiest, the Jesuit
missionary ; there are still finer bronze castings,
modelled, it is supposed, after Tycho Brahe's instruments. The same day we visited the great
Examination Hall, or yard. Each candidate is during
the three days' examination confined to his own cell,
in which he works, eats, and sleeps. These cells, of
which there are many thousands, are arranged in rows,
and form long and very narrow alleys. All official
appointments are reached by way of examination,
public and competitive. Among other places of

interest visited by us, I may mention the Hall of the Classics. In the cloisters which flank the two sides of the court are two hundred stone slabs, on which the whole of the Confucian classics are engraved.

One day we went out to a large Lama monastery called the Huang-sz, in the west court of which is a very fine white marble cenotaph, erected by the Emperor Chien-lung to the memory of a high lama, who ranked next after the Dalai Lama, or Pope of Thibet. Visiting Peking at the invitation of the emperor, he died while there of small-pox. His body was carried back to Thibet, but his clothes were buried under this monument, the right side of which is covered with sculptured representations of different scenes in his life. Every Mongol who visits Peking is expected to worship at this shrine. From this monastery we went to the great Bell Temple, in which is an immense bell, measuring fourteen feet in height, twenty-four feet round, and nine inches thick at the rim. It is a very wonderful piece of casting; it is completely covered inside and out with Chinese characters, extracts from the Buddhist classics, every character being as clear and sharply cut as if the bell had only been made yesterday. There is a similar bell in the Bell Tower, near the north gate of the Imperial city; it was made at the command of the Emperor Yunglo, and it is struck at midnight, to mark the time for the city watch. In connection with this bell a touching legend is told. 'Two attempts to cast this bell had failed. The emperor was enraged, and threatened Kuan-yin (the officer in charge) with death if he failed again. Kuan-yin's beautiful daughter, Ko-ai, heard the sad news, went to an astrologer to learn the fate of the next casting, and was told that that also would fail unless a virgin's blood was mixed with the ingredients. Ko-ai begged permission to see the next casting. The fateful moment came—the seething metal was poured out ; Ko-ai stepped forward, and crying, " For my father ! " threw herself headlong into the molten stream. One of the spectators rushed forward to seize her, but was only in time to catch one of her shoes, which came off in his hand. The horror-stricken father would have followed, but was held back by strong hands, and then led away a raving maniac. The casting was a complete success ; the bell was perfect, but no vestige of Ko-ai could be seen—only whenever the bell is struck there is a cry as of a female voice saying, " Hsie, hsie ! " (shoe, shoe). It is Ko-ai calling for her lost shoe.'

One day, through the kindness of one of the foreign professors, we had the opportunity of looking over the Imperial College. The college buildings are in the rear of the Tsung-li-Yamen, which, being literally translated, means the office for ruling all affairs—we should call it the Foreign Office. The students in the college are for the most part looking forward to the diplomatic service. The college is a small affair, but it may develop into something larger and better. Here, as elsewhere, we have the thin edge of Western science and civilization penetrating the hard crust of Chinese self-complacency and conservatism. Peking, not being one of the treaty ports, is not open to foreigners as a place of residence, and the only foreign residents are the members of the different Legations, those employed in the Customs' service, and a considerable band of missionaries of different denominations ; and the only foreign business in Peking is a store kept by a Dane, near the foreign Legations, and which is allowed to be carried on for their benefit.

During our stay in Peking our time was almost entirely occupied in inspecting the missionary work carried on there, and we managed to visit and see something of every mission in the city, both Protestant and Roman Catholic. We were the guests of Dr. Blodget, the senior missionary in Peking, connected with the American Board of Commissioners for Foreign Missions. The American Board is undenominational in its character and construction, and its history has been very similar to that of the London Missionary Society. After a time the Presbyterians and Methodists separated from it, establishing missions of their own, so that now, while theoretically undenominational, it is practically sustained and controlled by the Congregationalists. Dr. Blodget, who has been working in China for thirty-six years, did not begin regular and residential work in Peking till 1864, when, through the timely assistance of the late Dr. Wells Williams, the present mission premises were secured and a chapel opened for the public preaching of the Gospel. This was a new departure for Peking, and one that attracted crowds of curious listeners. At the commencement of this work, Dr. Blodget was assisted by the late Rev. W. C. Burns, who has left behind so fragrant a memory. The work is now carried on in two districts of the city, Dr. Blodget having charge of the Domestic and South Street Chapels, and his colleague, Rev. W. S. Amant, having charge of the North Street Chapel and country work. The chapels are open daily. I went into the South Street Chapel one afternoon, and found between forty and fifty men present, listening with apparent interest to the preaching of a native. Dr. Blodget has a daily morning class for the benefit of helpers and inquirers, while during the winter Mr. Amant and Mr. Aiken have a number of men under instruction.

There is an important educational work carried on. There are two boys' day schools and a girls' boarding school, founded many years ago by Mrs. Bridgman, and called the Bridgman School. This school has thirty-six pupils—bright, intelligent-looking girls—and is under the able management of Miss Chapin, who has been working here since 1872. There is a good work carried on in this mission among the women. There is also a mission press—the only one, I believe, north of Shanghai. This is under the management of Dr. Blodget, and I think that, with so good an office and plant, the Board would be wise to utilize them to a larger extent than they do at present.

The mission of the Methodist Episcopal Church occupies very large premises, the largest Protestant mission premises in Peking. They go in strongly for educational work, and have obtained from America a charter for establishing an institution, which is to be distinguished by the somewhat ambitious title of the Peking University. We are told that the proposal to found a university in Peking will arouse American enthusiasm, and call forth American liberality, as a more modest proposal would not. At present the institution is smaller than its name. It is doing good and useful work, but not on what are commonly regarded as university lines. We must not, however, despise the day of small things. Rome was not built in a day. They have good boys' and girls' schools, and important medical work is carried on by Dr. and Mrs. Dr. Jones. The evangelistic work has two centres, one in the north, the other in the south of the city. This mission is conducted under the superintendence of the Rev. H. A. Lowry, an able and energetic man.

The London Missionary Society is doing a good work in Peking. It was commenced in 1861 by Dr. Lockhart and the Rev. Dr. Edkins. This mission carries on its work in two districts of the city. The East City Mission is under the care of the Rev· G. Owen, and the chapel is the largest of all the Protestant places of worship in Peking. There is a boys' school, and also a boarding-school for the daughters of converts, in this branch of the mission. The West City Mission is under the care of the Rev. S. E. Meech ; the Rev. J. Stonehouse has charge of the country work. In the East City Mission there is very valuable hospital and dispensary work done under the care of Dr. E. T. Pritchard, while in the west some dispensing work is done by Miss Pearson. I gather from the 1889 report that three hundred and nineteen in-patients were treated, and that nearly 20,000 visits were paid by out-patients to the dispensary. There is a strong appeal for funds for the reconstruction of the hospital buildings, which are in an unsanitary condition, and for extending medical mission work in the west city. From what I saw I should say the appeal has not been made too soon, and I hope it will secure the needed funds.

The American Presbyterians carry on their work in two different parts of the city, north-east and north-west, and they too are doing good work—educational, medical, and evangelistic. We also visited the mission of the S P.G. This is the smallest and least important of the missions in Peking. It is a pity that it should shut itself off from all kinds of religious association with the other Protestant communities of the city.

The Roman Catholics, who have been in China some three hundred years, have a very considerable number of adherents, and their ecclesiastical edifices are among the most noticeable buildings in Peking. There is a fine church in the part of the city in which we dwelt, the interior of which is very grandly decorated. The towers rise high above the roofs of all surrounding buildings, and were often useful to us as landmarks. There is also a cathedral in the north-east of the Manchu city, to which we paid a visit. It was erected a few years ago, in the place of an older building, which was near to the emperor's residence; its proximity giving great offence, it was at last purchased by the Chinese Government, who gave the Roman Catholics the site for the present cathedral and the large establishment connected with it, with a very large sum of money—more than enough to cover all their outlay. We were conducted over the cathedral and the large educational establishment attached to it by a very courteous French priest, who knew enough English to make his meaning plain, and who seemed delighted to see visitors from Europe.

There is another cathedral of greater historical interest, known as the Portuguese Cathedral, which has been standing some two hundred years, and in connection with which educational and hospital work is carried on. Here we were treated very courteously, and our visit was regarded as a welcome one. We were much impressed by the self-denying Sisters who had charge of the hospital, which accommodates one hundred patients. On the afternoon we were there, a young Englishman, who had come up from Tien-tsin on business, was lying ill of small-pox. He was a Roman Catholic, we were told; but two of our party, hearing he was an Englishman, went in to see him. He was nearly unconscious then; he died that night, and was buried before noon the next day. From what we saw, we are sure that he received every attention. However strongly we may dissent from Roman Catholic doctrines, we cannot but admire these deeds of mercy.

One day we went out to see what is known as the Portuguese Cemetery, which is a little way outside one of the west gates of the city. It is the place where Ricci, Schaal, Verbiest, and other great Jesuit missionaries lie buried. Here, too, an educational work is carried forward, and preparations were being made for building a new church.

CHAPTER X.

AN INTERVIEW WITH LI-HUNG-CHANG.

Return to Tien-tsin—A rough ride—Tung-chow—American Board
Mission—Its educational work—Down the Peiho in a Chinese
boat—Good Friday in Tien-tsin—Arrangements for interview with
the viceroy—Courtesy of Lo-Fung-lu—Reception at the Yamen—
Interview with Li-Hung-Chang—Cordial welcome—Careful and
minute inquiries as to mission work—Reference to Roman Catholic
Missions—Inquiries as to opium traffic, and the relations of the
missionaries to it—The conduct of the British Government in
respect of it—Medical missions—The viceroy's strong approval ot
them—His wish that more medical missionaries might be sent out
—Departure from Tien-tsin.

AFTER a very pleasant stay in Peking we set out on
our way once again on Saturday, March 21. We
started on that day in order that we might spend
a Sunday at Tung-Chow, an important mission
station of the American Board. Tung-Chow, which
is really the port of Peking, is a large and important
place, with a population of 100,000. It is on the
Peiho, and an immense quantity of merchandise is
brought up as far as this by Chinese boats of small
draught and considerable burden. The goods are
here unshipped, and conveyed by cart, barrow, and
otherwise to Peking, over the stone road. Persons
travelling between Tung-chow and Tien-tsin usually

travel by the house-boats, which in large numbers ply on this part of the river.

It is a very important mission centre, in connection with which a large and varied work is carried on. There is a theological school, or college for the training of young men for the ministry, boys' and girls' schools, daily preaching in the street chapel, and a very good work among the women. The educational work is that for which this mission is chiefly distinguished—it is the educational centre of the American Board's Mission in North China. The last report of the American Board, speaking of the educational work at this station, says, 'We may hope to raise up a body of educated, clever young men, as preachers and teachers, fitted for any of the emergencies of the Church of Christ in China in the future.'

On Monday morning, soon after eight o'clock, we embarked for our voyage to Tien-tsin ; the distance is about seventy miles by road and a hundred and twenty by water. This was our first experience of river travelling. We engaged what is called a house-boat—a flat-bottomed vessel about forty-three feet long, ten feet wide in the widest part, tapering to four feet six inches fore and aft. In the centre of the boat is the house, which consists of three apartments of the width of the boat, less a narrow footway on either side of about twelve inches. As neither servants nor sailors knew a word of English, one could speak without restraint, though every word said in one apartment is distinctly heard in the next. These vessels, with a fair wind, use a large rectangular sail, which is kept distended by means of splines of bamboo, which run across at intervals of about eighteen inches ; if there is no wind, or a contrary wind, they are worked by means of a peculiar kind of scull, the long and broad blade of which is lashed at a very obtuse angle to a long handle, which is slung on an upright fixed in the boat's side. This imparts to it a semicircular motion. Used by strong and skilful hands, it is a very effective means of propulsion, and is everywhere used in the East—we saw it in the Sandwich Islands, Japan, Corea, and it is used everywhere in China. Two of these were worked in the fore part of our little vessel, and one aft. We had a strong head wind nearly all the way —for some hours it blew a gale, so that we had to lay up. We reached Tien-tsin about 6.30 on the Wednesday evening ; with a favourable wind we should have reached our destination the night before.

Most of our time in Tien-tsin was spent in paying hasty visits to those friends by whom we were so kindly entertained during our longer stay in November last. When we were in Tien-tsin before, it was suggested that it would be well that we should have an interview with Li-Hung-Chang, the Viceroy of Chih-li and the Grand Secretary of the Empire— by far the most important and influential man in China, after the emperor. He may be fairly spoken of as the Prime Minister of China. We of course said that we should be very pleased to have an interview with the viceroy, should he express himself willing to receive us. In November his time and ours was so much occupied that an interview could not be arranged. Our friend Mr. Richard, however, knowing that we should return through Tien-tsin, made arrangements for an interview with his excellency, through Loh-Fung-lu, the Secretary of the Admiralty, and private secretary to Li-Hung-Chang. We first of all called on Loh-Fung-lu, and had a long and very interesting conversation with him. He has visited England, and would like to visit it again ; he speaks good English, though with some deliberation, as one who is looking about for the exact phrase, which he nearly always gets. He is a great reader of Western, and especially English literature, has a taste for science, and if he does not belong to, he inclines towards the Herbert Spencer school of thought. He has made a study of the religions of the world, and regards Christianity as one of the most important factors of Western civilization. He treated us with great consideration. For instance, our interview was fixed for 5 p.m. He found, however, that two important Chinese deputations were to await upon the viceroy immediately before that time, and would probably delay our reception ; so he called to inform us of the fact, that we might not be kept waiting at the Yamen, and he remained for us, keeping up an interesting conversation till it was time to go, when he set off in his official chair, with his attendants, and we in our swifter but less dignified jinrickshas.

We reached the Yamen two or three minutes before the great man, and arriving in so undignified a way, were received with supercilious indifference by the crowd of servants who thronged its portal, and our friend Mr. Richard could scarcely get an answer to his inquiries as to the proper way of entrance. It was amusing to see how this almost insolent superciliousness was instantly changed into solicitous and almost servile attention when these subordinate officials saw Loh-Fung-lu step out of his chair, and at once cross the courtyard to welcome us, and take us under his own charge.

The Yamen, *i.e.* the official residence of the viceroy, is an immense establishment, consisting of many courtyards, surrounded with buildings that are used as offices and dwellings, forming altogether quite a little town. We passed through several courtyards, and along several corridors, and at last came to the private apartments of the viceroy, where we were shown into a very plainly furnished waiting-room, with uncarpeted floor. All round the room were seats covered with red cloth, and divided every few feet by broad elbow-rests, which serve as small tables for the waiting guests. Almost immediately after our arrival, servants came in and placed cups of tea at our side, and matches, should any wish to smoke. Then a very grand officer of state came in, a kind of chamberlain, I should think, who was introduced to us by Loh-Fung-lu, and remained in conversation for a few minutes. He took our cards, and made a number of inquiries—whom we were, and what we had been doing in China, and then retired, conveying the information thus obtained to the viceroy. After a few minutes had passed, another officer made his appearance, whose duty it was to conduct us into his excellency's presence.

L

After passing through another room and a long corridor, we came to two rooms connected by a large opening in the intervening wall, such as would be occupied in England with folding doors. As soon as our names were announced the viceroy came into the outer room and cordially welcomed us, shaking us by the hand quite in English fashion, and then himself conducting us to seats, which had been placed for us on either side of the table, at the head of which he sat. These rooms were somewhat sparsely furnished. The outer and larger one was lighted with Chinese lanterns, and the furniture was partly Chinese and partly American and European. The inner room (the viceroy's private room) was furnished throughout in foreign style—the floor covered with a Brussels carpet; there was one gas pendant with two lights, and several European lamps; oil paintings hung on the walls, of no great value. Li-Hung-Chang sat in an easy-chair at the head of the table, and we sat close to him on either side. Soon after we were seated, tea was again served, and cigarettes for those who liked to smoke. His excellency took one, but soon had his water-pipe brought in, his servant holding it by his side, and he taking an occasional puff. He kept plying us with questions as to our mission, our missionaries, ourselves, why we had come out, what we had seen, where we had been, and what were our general impressions of the country, the people, and the work which we had come out to inspect. The questions were those of a shrewd, clever man, accustomed to deal with men and things. Had our society head-quarters in London? Who were the directors? How were they appointed? Had the English Government anything to do with us, or we with it? Were we subsidized by the Government or by any public fund?

He seemed to have some difficulty in understanding how large numbers of people should band themselves together and subscribe what seems, even to a rich Chinaman, an immense sum of money to send out missionaries. We told him that we believed that the Gospel had done more for us as a country than anything else, and that we wished that China and the other nations of the world should share as largely as possible the blessings which we enjoyed. He inquired if we had anything to do with Roman Catholics, or sustained any kind of relations to them. We assured him that we had no relations with them, and strongly disapproved of very much in Roman Catholicism. He told us that he understood as much before, but that he was very glad to receive that assurance from our lips. He said that he knew intimately many provinces of China, and that, so far as his knowledge extended, the Roman Catholics had excited very strong prejudices against themselves, but he believed that the Protestant missionaries were good men, anxious to do good. We told him that it was the wish of our society to avoid all occasions of friction between themselves and the Chinese authorities, and that we believed that the attitude of our missionaries was conciliatory: we felt sure that good Christians would be good subjects. He then told us that he had received a deputation some time before presenting two numerously signed petitions against the opium traffic, and he asked us if those petitions had originated in any way with our society. We said that the petitions had not originated with us, but that the friends and supporters of our society were strongly opposed to the use of opium, and were anxious to do all that could be done to lessen its use. He said, 'You have been in Shansi, where opium is very largely consumed; what do you think of the effects of it, so far as you have observed them?' We replied that it was impossible for any one to visit the province, even for so short a time as we did, without feeling that opium was a great curse, and that we had constantly met with those who were evidently its victims; and, so far as we had conversation with the people, those who took opium admitted it to be an evil, though their will-power was so enfeebled by its use that they felt themselves to be powerless to shake off the habit. He asked us what was the attitude of our missionaries in respect of its use. We said it was one of absolute and uncompromising opposition, and that no opium-smoker was allowed to be a member of our Churches. He then asked if our missionaries had been really successful in saving any from this habit. We told him they had, and that, from all that we could hear, nothing but the Gospel was potent enough to deal with this evil. Then he asked how we knew that those Church members who professed to have abandoned the habit did not secretly indulge in it. We replied that the habit was such that it could scarcely be kept a secret, and that where any lapse became known the offender was subjected to the discipline of the Church.

The conversation then turned upon the conduct of the British Government in reference to the opium trade, and especially their conduct in forcing opium upon the Chinese. We freely admitted that we regarded the conduct of England in this matter as indefensible, and assured him that an ever-increasing number of people at home looked back upon it with feelings of shame and regret. The viceroy said that he was glad to hear that we took so just a view of the question, and somewhat satirically added that, as we were sending out missionaries to convert the Chinese, we might try to convert our own Government. We told him that public opinion was being educated on this question, and that we quite hoped to convert the Government. He laughed, and said he supposed that there was the money difficulty in the way, and that it was always hard to convince a government of the propriety of relinquishing a certain source of income, however questionable its moral character might be. We were then asked our opinion as to medical missions. We told him that we had been greatly pleased by what we had seen of their work, and that, viewed in relation to our evangelistic enterprise, it had rendered valuable service in lessening prejudice, and that anti-foreign feeling which was so formidable an obstacle to the spread of the Gospel.

The viceroy seemed pleased when I told him that I had read the preface which he had written for Dr. Hunter's translation of the *British Pharmacopœia,* upon which he said that he valued very highly the labours of medical missionaries, but wanted to know if we could secure the services of first-class medical men at the salaries we paid. We replied that they were missionaries as well as medical men, and that they came out, not to make money, but to render service to a cause to which they were prepared to sacrifice the prospects and possibilities of money-making. The viceroy then said, 'We are Confucianists—that is good for us ; you are Christians—that is good for you. We Confucianists think that we are able to look after our own souls, but we cannot so well look after our own bodies. Our native doctors do not know much about our bodies, but your foreign doctors know a great deal, and I hope that you will send out a great many more medical missionaries.' We said that we quite hoped to send out more medical missionaries, but that they would feel it was their work to heal the souls of men as well as their bodies.

Towards the close of our visit champagne was served to those who liked to take it. The viceroy kept his glass before him untouched for some time ; at last he raised it to his lips, bowing to each of us. This was evidently the sign that the interview was at at end. Loh-Fung-lu almost immediately afterwards intimated that we were obliged to take our departure. The viceroy rose and accompanied us to the outer door of his private apartments, bidding us farewell with more English hand-shaking, telling us that he valued the information as to missionary work which we had given him. He is a fine-looking man, tall and somewhat spare. We were told before we went that we were not to be surprised if we found him somewhat brusque in his manner—to us he was exceedingly courteous. Our interview with him lasted more than an hour and a quarter.

One peculiarity of the interview—it is a thing at least which strikes a foreigner as peculiar—was the freedom with which servants and subordinate officials seemed to claim the right of seeing everything that went on, and hearing everything that was said. In the anteroom there was a little crowd of interested spectators, who watched every movement and heard every word spoken. They gathered as soon as we had taken our seats, and silently dispersed as soon as the sign was given that the audience was at an end. I sat where I had a full view of them.

As we were to sail before daybreak next morning, we went on board the Hsin-yu, the steam-vessel which was to take us to Shanghai. We called at Chefoo for two or three hours, and got on board some luggage, which we left there in the autumn. We had a slow and rather rough passage—a strong head wind and heavy seas—and our flat-bottomed vessel, when lifted by these heavy seas, plumped down again in such a way as nearly to jerk us out of our berths. We, however, at last reached Shanghai, though nearly a day later than we should have arrived had the weather been favourable.

CHAPTER XI.

SHANGHAI.

Shanghai—The Yang-tze-Kiang—The first view of Shanghai—Apparent
wealth and prosperity—Municipal council—The Anglo-Chinese
town—Important missionary centre—St. Luke's Hospital—Chinese
hospital—American Presbyterian Mission Press—Union Church—
Native city—Departure for Hankow—The Yang-tze-Kiang—The
changes in the river-bed — Nanking — River-Scenery — Water-
buffaloes.

LONG before we reached Shanghai, the discoloured
state of the water reminded us that we were approaching the mouth of the Yang-tze-Kiang, one of the
great rivers of the world, and which places within
reach of the coast immense districts of Central and
Western China. After entering the river, there is
for a long way but little to interest the passenger
beyond the enormous stretch of yellowish-brown
water, faintly outlined, where the coast is visible, by
low-lying land, hardly distinguishable from the river
which it bounds. After steaming up the Yang-tze-
Kiang for some distance, we came to the mouth of
the Hwang-poo, on which Shanghai is situated.
Having a small draught, we had no difficulty in
crossing the bar at Woosung, and we pursued our

voyage without interruption for about ten miles,
when we were unmistakably reminded that, though
we were on a Chinese river, we were drawing near to
a great foreign settlement. As we moved on we met
with multiplying proofs of the fact that Western, and
especially British, wealth, energy, and enterprise had
been doing their accustomed work.

Shanghai, approached by the river, presents a very
striking appearance, and there are many things so
home-like that one can scarcely believe that it is a
Chinese river. But, amid all the signs of Western
civilization, there are many things to convince you
that you are in China still. The Hwang-poo, though
small compared with the great river of which it is an
affluent, is a very fine body of water, and as you draw
near to Shanghai you have a long stretch of it before
you, crowded with craft of many different nationalities,
large numbers of native junks, and some ocean-going
steamers and foreign men-of-war, while for miles
along one bank there runs what is called the Bund—
the river frontage of the foreign settlements. Beyond
the wharves and jetties immediately adjacent to the
river there is a finely kept public road, which always
presents a busy scene, with crowds of coolies carrying
their heavy burdens on bamboo poles—nearly all
the porterage is done in this way—innumerable
jinrickshas, and private and public carriages.

Beyond the roadway is a long line of splendid
buildings, stretching in either direction as far as eye
can reach—warehouses such as are seen in London,
Liverpool, or Glasgow ; banks, offices of different
shipping companies, and of great firms of merchants ;

buildings that are palatial in their appearance ; while
on one part of the Bund are some well-kept public
gardens, with hothouses and conservatories. All this
met our eyes and filled us with astonishment and
admiration as we slowly steamed up to our landing-
stage, which was at the upper part of the Bund. As
we drew near to it we were invaded by a perfect
swarm of coolies, who came out in sampans, and
climbed up the ship's sides like squirrels. Some were
touting for hotels and boarding-houses ; most of them
were eagerly offering their services as porters. The
landing-stage and wharf were crowded with coolies,
and interested or disinterested spectators, and we
were very glad to distinguish in the crowd the friends
who had come down to meet and welcome us.

There are three foreign settlements in Shanghai,
stretching along the river front—the British, with the
American on the one side and the French on the other,
the British being the largest, most important, and most
prosperous. In 1842 Shanghai was seized by the
British, but not permanently occupied as a possession
of the Crown, and from that time large numbers of
foreigners, chiefly British, settled down there for
trading purposes—first of all in the native city, but,
after a few years, removing to the more salubrious site
on which the foreign settlement gradually grew up,
until it has attained its present vast proportions. Without any formal treaty, I believe, the Chinese authorities
have quietly recognized the three settlements which
I have named—the British, American, and French.

Public affairs in the British and American settlements are managed by a sort of municipal council,

which is annually elected. The roads are well kept, the sanitary arrangements are satisfactory, the streets are lighted with gas-lamps, and with supplementary electric lighting ; there is a well-organized police force, with a small number of Europeans and a large number of Chinese and Sikhs as constables. The Chinese police wear a uniform very much like the European, but with a slight conformity to Chinese ideas and usages, while the nationality of the Sikh policeman is indicated by a voluminous and picturesque red turban. There is also a considerable and well-disciplined volunteer force—cavalry, artillery, and infantry. Shanghai also boasts of a very effective fire brigade.

In connection with the foreign settlement, there has grown up a very large Anglo-Chinese town, with a population at present of more than 200,000. This densely populated town forms part of the settlement, and is subject to the control of the municipal council, and its inhabitants doubtless feel that the police and sanitary regulations that are imposed, and the taxes they have to pay, constitute but a small price for the manifold advantages they enjoy under foreign protection and control. As you walk these crowded streets you have much to remind you that you are in what is virtually a Chinese town, but it is the cleanest Chinese town you have ever seen, and this enormous population, which has voluntarily placed itself under foreign authority, is as orderly and law-observing as can be desired.

Shanghai is an important missionary centre, and a large number of missionaries are resident here carrying on work in the city and its neighbourhood. In Shanghai, as the port of entrance, the China Inland Mission has a large establishment, which I visited, and where I made the acquaintance of the Rev. Hudson Taylor, the able manager of this great missionary movement. I also saw the work carried on at the St. Luke's Hospital, which is in connection with the American Episcopal Church. I was shown over it by Dr. Boone, the superintending surgeon, and brother of Bishop Boone. It is, I think, on the whole, one of the best-equipped hospitals I have seen in China. In 1890, five hundred and twelve in-patients and 21,290 out-patients were treated, at a total cost, not reckoning salaries, of less than 2000 taels,[1] which sum, with nine hundred taels put down for repairs and building, was raised by subscriptions from foreigners and natives without trenching on mission funds. Dr. Boone told me that all the money needed for carrying on the hospital was thus obtained without difficulty. Another hospital which I visited is known as the Chinese Hospital. The building is in connection with the London Missionary Society's property, but the work is carried on under the management of an independent committee, and the expenses are met by independent subscriptions. In 1890, eight hundred and twenty-six in-patients were treated, while 23,781 out-patients were treated in the dispensary practice. It is carried on at a cost of a little over 2000 taels per annum. The religious work in this hospital is in the hands of the representatives of the London Mission. The American

---

[1] A tael is of variable value = to about 5*s.*

Presbyterian Mission maintains a very important printing establishment. Last year they issued 552,395 copies of different publications, with a total of 37,750,625 pages. It is under very careful and effective management. Many of the workmen are members of the Church ; they carry on a Thursday afternoon prayer-meeting among themselves. At one of these I was present, and gave an address. The American Methodist Episcopal Mission carries on an extensive educational work, which I had the opportunity of inspecting. The evangelistic work carried on by the different missions is similar in character to that which I have referred to as going on in other centres. On the afternoon of the Sunday I spent in Shanghai, at the invitation of the Rev. W. Muirhead, I attended a native service in connection with the London Mission. The large chapel was filled, and the congregation was an interesting one. One day I called at the Street Chapel in the native city, but not at the hour of service. They have a good attendance there every day. There was much other work which I should have been glad to visit had my time allowed. On the Sunday I preached morning and evening at the Union Church, of which the Rev. T. R. Stevenson is the pastor. It is a handsome building, and there is a good congregation. On the following Monday I had the pleasure of meeting all, or nearly all, the missionaries of Shanghai at their weekly prayer-meeting, and gave, at their request, an account of our travels in China, and my impressions of missionary work.

On the Monday night I went on board the Kiang-yu, a fine vessel of 2000 tons, belonging to the China Merchants Company, built for service on the Yang-tze-Kiang river, and arranged to carry a heavy cargo and a large number of Chinese passengers, with very good accommodation for a small number of saloon passengers, who are for the most part Europeans or Americans. We were obliged to embark over-night, as she was to start before daylight the next morning. Our saloon party was small—a young lady belonging to the Presbyterian Mission, who was going up to Nanking; an Irish gentleman, a Commissioner of Customs; the Archimandrite of the Greek Church in China; and an old Chinese gentleman, who had been in England, and could speak very good English, and who turned out to be the father-in-law of a young Chinaman with whom we had become quite friendly in our voyage from San Francisco to Yokohama. These were the visible saloon passengers, but besides these one or two cabins were occupied by well-to-do Chinamen and their wives, of whom we saw scarcely anything during the voyage.

The Yang-tze-Kiang, which is navigated by steam-boats for about 1100 miles, is a magnificent river, and in its broad expanse seems more like an arm of the sea than a river. You are impressed by the magnitude of the mighty flood which it is ever pouring into the sea ; but beyond that there is little to interest, the land on either side being flat and monotonous. After a while the river narrows, and we pass a great peach-growing district, and for a long distance look upon an almost unbroken mass of peach-blossom. The trees seemed to be comparatively small, but were clothed with bloom and growing quite near to the water's edge. We stop successively at Tung-chow, Kiangwin, and Tin-sen-chow—places that are mere names to me, but which are full of interest to many of my fellow-voyagers.

We then come to Chin-Kiang, one of the treaty ports and a great depôt for tea. Here we drop a good many of our Chinese passengers, and take in a good many more. Some distance from the river is Golden Island, which was originally an isolated rock covered with temples and a slender pagoda on its summit. In 1823 it was an island on the north shore; in 1842 it was in the centre of the river, and our fleet sailed round it on its way up to Nanking; it is now on the south bank two miles from the shore. This serves to illustrate the changes that are ever taking place in the bed of the Yang-tze, and which render its navigation uncertain and often perilous. The leadsman never ceases from his work, and I am getting quite used to the monotonous and melancholy cry with which he announces the number of fathoms. We gradually work up the river against a strong tide and a stronger headwind till we come to Nanking. It was once, for a time, the actual capital of the entire empire, and a place of great commercial prosperity and political importance. It is, if we have regard to history, one of the famous cities of China. It was taken possession of by the British in 1842, and suffered much in the Tai-ping rebellion. The enclosed space is of vast extent, the circuit of the walls being some twenty-five miles. We sailed within a short distance of its southern wall for miles, but it seemed to enclose nothing but wild and uncultivated country—not a house being visible. The inhabited part of the city enclosure was quite out of view, on the other side of some low hills.

After leaving Nanking, the river scenery becomes much more varied and beautiful, improving as we proceed; fine ranges of hills or mountains coming into view in the distance, while rising immediately from the river are grass-covered hills or precipitous rocks. In one place there rises up in the midst of the river a small but exceedingly beautiful island of rock, called the Little Orphan. This mass of rock, which rears itself to a considerable height almost precipitously, is clothed to a large extent with luxuriant vegetation, and seems to be the chosen home of a large number of river-birds—fishing-hawks and cormorants—many of which were sweeping round it as we passed. On this very small island is a temple, with several priests, who go out in their sampans and ask for contributions from the junks that go up and down the river. The little island, in the glow of the evening sun, with the swift river eddying round its base, and a perfect swarm of swift-winged birds sweeping round its summit, forms one of the most beautiful pictures to be seen in China.

After leaving Nanking, we stop at Wuhu, Tatung, Ngan-Kin, and then come to Kiu-Kiang, a treaty port through which nearly all our green tea reaches us, and which is also the most important centre of the Chinese porcelain trade. As we do not reach Kiu-Kiang till 10.20 p.m., I can see little beyond the two hulks which form the very convenient floating wharves of this port. As we move up stream the river scenery improves, and in many parts is exceedingly beautiful—cliffs and precipitous bluffs of considerable height—the limestone rocks being often broken into very striking and picturesque forms. Many of these were on the more even surfaces clothed with a greensward brightened in places with many-coloured mosses and lichens, while at the back, some miles away, were fine ranges of hills or mountains rising to a height of 2000 or 3000 feet. The rock scenery was almost exclusively on the south side of the river, the bank on the other side being but little raised above the river level, and on that side there stretched away an immense plain—well cultivated and fertile—though here and there we could distinguish at a distance considerable elevations. The ground on this side was brilliant with the vivid green of early spring, while large spaces were covered with rape, beautiful just now with its bright yellow and honey-scented blossom.

Many sights of interest engaged the attention. A large number of persons were fishing, in boats and on bamboo stages projecting from the shore, and employing in their calling a great many ingenious contrivances, such as only a Chinaman would think of. In many places we saw men engaged in burning the limestone rock. They do not build kilns such as we are familiar with, but they have a huge basket arrangement, within which the pieces of limestone are piled up, with an excavation for a furnace at the bottom. In other places men were digging out, not coal, but a coarse shale, which is used by them for

M

fuel.   I was told that there is some very good iron obtainable from the neighbouring hills.   I also saw on the banks animals I had never seen before, called water-buffaloes.   They seem to be almost amphibious in their habits, and are largely used in rice cultivation. As we drew near to Hankow the river-banks became less interesting, though the immediate approach to Hankow is very fine, the river being fully a mile wide. Hankow, with its beautiful Bund lying on one side, Wuchang, a large city on the other side of the Yang-tze, and beyond, on the same side as Hankow, but separated from it by the river Han, the large and populous city of Hanyang, forming jointly one of the most important centres of population in China.

CHAPTER XII.

HANKOW, HONG-KONG, AND CANTON.

I SPENT four days very pleasantly at Hankow,
during which time I was the guest of the Rev. Arnold
Foster, of the London Mission. The river opposite
the Bund is at least a mile wide, and looking up the
river you see it crowded with Chinese junks and
sampans, and on the same side as the Bund the native
cities of Hankow and Hanyang, separated by the
large river Han, which here joins the Yang-tze, and

on the other side of the Yang-tze is the city of
Wuchang. These three cities, which have grown up
on the banks of the two rivers, while separate as civic
communities, form one great centre of population, and
it is, or has been, one of the most important commercial centres of the empire. The population of
the three cities has been very variously estimated ;
we probably should not be very far out if we were to
put it at something between a million and a million
and a quarter. Remembering how closely the poor
Chinese herd together, no one can look upon these
cities without feeling that they contain an immense
number of people. Besides those who dwell in the
cities and suburbs, there is a very large boat population : the river Han presents the appearance of a
perfect forest of masts.

One afternoon, in company with Mr. Foster, I
ascended Hanyang Hill, from the summit of which
a very remarkable view is obtained. The country
for many miles round is flat and uninteresting, and
in the flood season to a large extent under water.
Through this plain you can see the mighty river
Yang-tze running in a north-easterly and south-
westerly direction, till it is lost in the dim distance,
while from the north-west you can trace the river
Han, as it pursues its tortuous course, till it divides
the cities of Hanyang and Hankow (Hanmouth),
emptying itself into the Yang-tze, while on the
other side of this larger river, at the distance of
a little more than a mile, there spreads out within
walls that you can distinctly trace the large and
populous city of Wuchang, the monotony of the

plain being broken here and there by hills of inconsiderable size. From this hill you see these three cities, separated from one another by two rivers, forming one great centre of population and commercial activity like New York, Brooklyn, and New Jersey. From this hill we looked down upon what must be regarded in China as a strange spectacle— the preparations which are being made on a very large scale for the establishment of iron-works. Many acres of ground between the foot of the hill and the river Han have been enclosed by lofty and carefully constructed embankments, to protect the works from the summer floods ; through this already runs a tramway. Large works are being erected under foreign superintendence, and large quantities of foreign machinery are being imported. There is plenty of iron ore on one side of Hankow, and plenty of coal on the other, and these works will be in a comparatively short time in full and, let us hope, successful operation. The viceroy is also starting a cotton-factory at Wuchang. An immense amount of money has been already sunk in them, the prime mover in this undertaking being the Viceroy of Hoopeh, H. E. Tsang—an intelligent and far-seeing man. He is a man much in advance of his countrymen, and is using his great influence not only in starting these works, but in projecting sundry railway and mining schemes, which if carried out will open up the country, and render available some of its magnificent and almost inexhaustible resources. He has thus awakened a great deal of interest, and what we trust will prove to be well-grounded expectation.

If from any cause he were removed, he might be followed by a man of a totally different stamp, and these great undertakings would be abandoned. All such movements, however, whether they issue in success or failure, have their value as breaking in upon Chinese conservatism.

I saw something of the native cities of Hankow and Hanyang, but nothing need be said concerning them except this, that they are as dirty and unsavoury as Chinese cities usually are. How a people laying claim to civilization can complacently accept such conditions of life, and go on from one generation to another without making any serious endeavour to amend them, is what a foreigner finds difficult to comprehend. But so it is, and so apparently it will be. You feel almost as though you were in a different world when you pass within the limits of the English Concession. It is a very little world—about half a mile long and a quarter of a mile deep, bounded on the river-side by the Bund, which, with its river frontage and well-grown and shade-giving trees, forms a pleasant promenade, much valued by the foreign community. The affairs are managed by a small municipal council, similar in its constitution and operation to the larger one at Shanghai. The roads are as well kept and lighted as those of an English town, and there is a native police force under foreign superintendence. A fine building, to be used as a police court and for other purposes, is now nearing completion.

Hankow is the great centre of the tea trade. Ku-Kiang seems to be the great collecting centre, and

Hankow the great tea mart ; there do tea-buyers for the tea-consuming people of the world congregate. Towards the middle of May the tea season commences, and from that time till it closes, a month or five weeks later, there is one constant and exciting rush of business ; everyone is working under high pressure. According, however, to common consent, the tea trade of Hankow is not what it used to be. Indian and Ceylon teas are to an ever-increasing extent taking the place of China teas in the English market, and are likely to do so more largely in the future, unless the Chinese are stirred up by declining trade to a more vigorous competition. In Hankow the Russian merchants seem to occupy the first place, and they hold completely in their own hands an important branch of the tea trade of which little is known in England. I allude to the manufacture of brick-tea—tea compressed into hard cakes and consumed in large quantities in Mongolia, Siberia, and some parts of North China. This brick-tea is not only an important article of commerce and consumption, but in the districts referred to a common medium of exchange. This business, which was formerly limited to small manufacturers in the country, is now carried on exclusively by large Russian firms, with all the appliances of Western machinery, at Hankow and Ku-Kiang. The presence of these huge manufactories is made known by a powerful and all-pervading odour, distinguishable in every part of the settlement. Just as in brewing towns like Romford or Burton you have everywhere the smell of beer, so here you have everywhere the smell of tea—not the delicate fragrance of fresh-made tea, but the smell that prevails in the kitchen of a school where tea in large quantities is being prepared for a school festival.

By the kindness of Dr. Griffith John, I was conducted over one of these large Russian factories, and I saw the process of manufacturing brick-tea from beginning to end, and was presented with a brick of tea as a memorial of my visit. I first of all went into a large room in which many men were at work making the wooden moulds into which the prepared tea is pressed, then to a room where the tea is reduced to a fine powder; this powder is then placed in bags, and these bags of tea-dust are placed in perforated metal cylinders, and exposed to the action of steam just long enough to become sufficiently moistened. The tea is then placed in the moulds and subjected to great pressure, coming out in appearance very much like a black paving-tile, about nine inches by six inches, and one inch thick or nearly so. They are then carefully examined; imperfect ones are thrown on one side to be ground up again; the others are dried and packed separately in paper, done up in neatly covered packages of sixty or seventy each, and in due course sent to North China, Siberia, and Mongolia. They also manufacture the same articles into small tablets, very much like our chocolate cakes. That part of the establishment, however, was not in work the day I was there. This factory employs about 1400 hands, and sends out about a quarter of a million of these larger bricks, and in addition a large number of tablets.

Among other places I visited was the large Italian Roman Catholic Mission School, which takes in, feeds, clothes, and educates some six hundred children. The lady superior, an Italian, speaking good English, received me most kindly. I told her that I had been visiting our own missions, and should like, while in Hankow, to see the work which was carried on under her superintendence. She said she should be pleased for me to see all there was to be seen, and she herself conducted me over the establishment. In one room there were a number of babies in cradles, in another a number of little things that had not long left the cradle behind. As soon as the children are old enough to use their fingers they are set to some useful employment, their work being arranged and graduated according to their ages and capacities. Take, for instance, the work with cotton. There were some poor blind women picking the cotton wool ; then there were girls spinning with the old-fashioned spinning-wheel that we now only see in pictures ; in other rooms you would see girls working at the hand-loom, making the cotton cloth so largely used for Chinese dress. Some were making tapes and towellings. A large number of the girls were engaged in crochet-work and lace-making—some exceedingly beautiful specimens of lace-work were shown me—while others were engaged embroidering silks and satins. Some splendid specimens intended for church decoration were exhibited, and some which were being made to order for the decoration of the rooms to be occupied by the Czarewitch during his anticipated visit to Hankow. A considerable sum is earned by the sale of lace and other things made in the mission school. The girls are taught to wash—to do household work of different kinds and cook ; the lady superior told me that sixteen girls were told off for the morning and sixteen for the afternoon cooking. At the back is a large pond or small lake, well stored with fish, and I saw on a projecting bamboo stage a girl busily engaged in catching fish. The lady superior called the young fisher-girl, who seemed very pleased to show me her good-sized basket well filled with fish, which were to be cooked for that day's dinner. The large dormitories are clean and well arranged. In passing through one large room I saw an old China woman busily engaged with shallow baskets, in which was a quantity of green material, which looked like chopped mint or spinach. She held out one of the baskets for my inspection, and I was about to take up a handful of the green stuff more closely to examine it, but was deterred by her look and cry of horror, and I found that the green stuff was carefully chopped mulberry-leaves, upon which a perfect swarm of little silkworms were feeding—in that stage of their existence not larger round than a medium-sized sewing-needle—and I was told that the large room would be fully occupied by them in the later stages of their existence. Altogether I spent a very pleasant time in this institution, and could not but admire the Christian benevolence of these good women who were so nobly devoting themselves to the service of these poor children in a strange land. It is an industrial rather than an educational establishment : the teaching only occupies two hours a day, and does not go beyond reading and religious instruction.

The Wesleyan Missionary Society carries on an important work in these three great cities of Hankow, Hanyang, and Wuchang—a work which stretches out for many miles into the country. While it is emphatically an evangelistic mission, it is doing some good educational work, although the Wuchang High School, which was started with the view of attracting the educated youth of the country, does not appear to have met with the success which its promoters anticipated, and which the conductors of that institution certainly deserve. I had the opportunity of looking at the work of the Wesleyan Mission in the native city of Hankow. They have been occupying that city for some years, and their work divides itself into three branches—evangelistic, educational, and medical—in connection with each of which they can point to good and encouraging results. They have commodious buildings which they hope by-and-by to extend. I was very much interested in a small blind school, in which about a dozen boys are educated on Braile's system. One boy wrote at dictation a sentence in about the same time it would have taken a sighted boy who wrote slowly and carefully. The writing is done by making indentations on a paper through slots in a brass ruler, which are of the size that the Chinese words should occupy, and the raised points on the other side are those by which the blind read. The medical work of this mission is carried on in recently erected and well-equipped hospitals, the male hospital being under the care of Dr. Hodge, and the female under that of Miss Sugden. This women's hospital has proved a very successful experiment, and we were assured that it is greatly valued by the Chinese women, who are glad to have the medical services of one of their own sex. The work began in a very simple way nearly thirty years ago, and was carried on for about fifteen years, and then for some years the medical work of the mission was dropped. It was recommenced in 1885, and now there are these two hospitals, which for character of accommodation and completeness of equipment can compare with any in China, the male hospital taking in twenty-five patients, and the female twenty-three. These hospitals have been provided, I believe, to a large extent by funds specially contributed. In connection with, and in addition to, this medical work is important evangelistic work, similar to that which I have so often described in connection with other missions.

The London Missionary Society has for a long time carried on a large and important work in these cities—a work which in the minds of many readers is inseparably associated with the name of Dr. Griffith John, who has for his colleagues the Revs. A. Foster, A. Bonsey, W. Owen, and C. G. Sparham, the medical work being under the care of Dr. Gillieson. The London Mission has been pre-eminently an evangelistic mission — as distinguished from some others which are more distinctively educational. Said Dr. John to me, ' Ours is a preaching mission.' After his long experience of nearly forty years he feels more strongly than ever that while other branches of work have their value, and should not be neglected, the strength of a mission should be given to the preaching of the Gospel, and he attaches the greatest importance to the work carried on daily in the street chapels. The inclemency of the weather did not allow me to see the ordinary week-day congregation at one of these chapels. The work done at them, I am told, is very encouraging in its character.

The medical work of this mission is carried on under the care of Dr. Gillieson, in connection with two hospitals. One is for men, capable of receiving a considerable number of patients ; and there is a small and beautiful women's hospital, called the Margaret Hospital, in memory of the late Mrs. John. Important evangelistic work is done in connection with the medical work.

On the afternoon of my last day in Hankow, I spent the time with a number of native preachers and helpers, who had assembled for a short conference, on lines similar to those on which our own Church leaders meet in Shantung. They were strong, intelligent, self-reliant men—just the kind of men we want to take the lead in the native churches. They were pleased to meet with me as representing the Christians of England, to whom they feel they owe so much. There are several schools maintained by this mission, and Mr. and Mrs. Foster have under their own care a small number of very interesting and promising Eurasian girls. Altogether this mission, placed as it is in an important centre of population, is one of great promise.

I had the opportunity of seeing the press of the Scottish Bible Society, which is under the able management of Mr. Archibald, who, though not a practical printer, has introduced a number of small inventions, which contribute to the economy and efficiency of the establishment.

We stopped at all the ports going down the river, and for some hours at Chin-Kiang. The British forces captured this place in 1842, and the Tai-ping rebels occupied it from 1853–1857. The city was almost destroyed by the rebels ere they evacuated it, and it has not yet recovered from the effects of that rebellion. The city lies between one of the entrances of the Grand Canal and the bank of the Yang-tze. Most of the houses are built on the level, but some are on the hill-slope, and viewed from the river it presents a pleasant and attractive appearance. The foreign settlement stretches along the river front from the Grand Canal, with the customary Bund and foreign-built houses and warehouses ; and, as at other points on this river, old P. and O. hulks form very convenient and commodious floating wharves. It was at one time anticipated that a very important trade would be developed here. These hopes were, however, for a time disappointed. The closing of the Grand Canal in 1853, when the Yellow River changed its lower course from the eastward to the northward, and the consequent interference with the through traffic between Peking and the great cities of the south, almost extinguished the trade of this port, while the opening of Hankow as a great tea-exporting centre interfered with it in another way. Of late years, I was told, the trade has been improving, notwithstanding these serious drawbacks.

I availed myself of the opportunity afforded by our short stay at this port of visiting the mission station. I saw first that connected with the China Inland Mission, and then that of the American Southern Baptists. There is also a mission of the American Methodist Episcopal Church, which I had not time to reach. There was a very serious riot in this place in the early part of 1889, when the British Consulate and many of the foreign residences were burnt down, and the residents had to escape for their lives. There seems to be a good missionary work doing here, and new and commodious buildings have taken the place of those which were destroyed.

I reached Shanghai on the Friday about noon, and late that night got on board the Hae-shin, which was to sail the next morning before dawn for Foo-chow.

In our voyage to Foo-chow we scarcely lost sight of China, or the islands that skirt its coast. These rocky islands are very numerous, forming quite an archipelago. The city of Foo-chow is situated on the left bank of the river Min, about thirty-four miles above the entrance. To this river there are three main approaches from the sea, and the navigation is exceedingly difficult, owing to the many rocks and strong currents. Sea-going vessels have to anchor at Losing Island, or, as it is generally called, Pagoda Island ; above that the river is only navigable by steam-launches and native craft drawing little water. On the river Min the scenery is more beautiful than anything which we have seen in China.

Foo-chow, the capital of Fu-Kien province, is nine

miles above the Pagoda Island entrance, where we had to transfer ourselves from the steamer to a small steam-launch. The port was opened to foreign commerce by the Treaty of Nanking. The native city is built on a plain, and is about three miles from the riverside, with which it is connected by immense suburbs, containing, I should say, a larger population than the walled city itself. The attention of foreigners was early directed to Foo-chow as a likely place for the shipment of Bohea tea. Before the port was opened, this was carried overland to Canton—a long, difficult, and expensive journey. As early as 1830 the East India Company made strong representations in favour of opening this port, but without effect; it remained closed till 1842. After the opening of the port but little business was done for some considerable time; but after a while the trade rapidly developed, and Foo-chow became one of the chief tea-ports of the empire.

The native city is built around three hills, and surrounded by a wall, the circuit of which is between six and seven miles; but though the streets are not less narrow and dirty than in other Chinese cities, the large number of fine-grown trees which adorn the grounds of private and official residences, and the well-wooded hills which rise up in the midst of the city, impart to it a pleasant and almost picturesque appearance. Near the east gate are several hot springs, which are used by the natives for skin diseases, and are believed to be efficacious. Let us hope that they are, for cutaneous affections are not less common here than in other places we have visited

A few miles above the city the river Min divides into two branches, which, after pursuing separate courses for fifteen miles, unite a little above the Pagoda anchorage.

The foreign settlement of Foo-chow stands on the northern side of the island thus formed, and is called by the natives Nantai. A long and narrow bridge connects the settlement with the suburbs and city on the other side of the river. A straight street, two miles and a half long, and not more than ten or twelve feet broad, runs from the bridge to the city gate. It is lined on either side with shops, many of them of a superior character, all of them open to the street, and in many of them you see artisans busily occupied with their respective handicrafts. The narrow thoroughfare, made narrower by the encroach-ments of the shops, is thronged to such an extent that it is difficult to make your way along, and when we passed through it presented one of the busiest and most striking street scenes that we have witnessed in China. The population of the city, suburbs, and settlement is estimated at 630,000. There is a dock, managed and owned by foreigners, and a patent slip at the Chinese Arsenal. Foo-chow is noted for the production of artificial flowers and birds, carving in wood and soap-stone, and for lacquer-work, which claims to be superior to the Japanese. The chief exports are tea, paper, oranges, and wood, but principally tea ; and now that the tea season is approaching, that is the most common and appa-rently the most interesting topic of conversation.

We called first of all upon Archdeacon Wolfe, by

N

whom we were most kindly received and entertained. The Church Missionary Society carries on a very important and most encouraging work, both educational and evangelistic. They have a women's school, a boys' school, a girls' school, and a training college for those who are looking forward to the Christian ministry, and the work in Foo-chow is merely the centre of a great work carried on in the Fu-Kien province for many miles around. Archdeacon Wolfe not only acted as our guide while we were inspecting the work of the Church Missionary Society, but rendered us the additional service of conducting us to and over that carried on by the American Methodist Episcopal Church, which here, as elsewhere in China, is distinctively an educational work, for the carrying on of which they are splendidly provided with buildings and all necessary equipment. These buildings have been almost entirely furnished by private donors, by far the largest benefaction having been received from a wealthy and converted Chinaman interested in the education of his countrymen. In the after part of the day the archdeacon's colleague, Mr. Lloyd, conducted us to the Mission of the American Board, at the head of which is Dr. Baldwin, one of the oldest missionaries in China. To reach this we had a chair ride of more than three miles through the street. This work is carried on within the walled city, and divides itself into three branches—evangelistic, educational, and medical; and our friends at this mission seem to have much to encourage them. We visited a large girls' boarding-school belonging to the Church Missionary Society, and were deeply interested in what we saw there, and then returned to spend a pleasant evening with Mr. and Mrs. Lloyd and one or two other mission workers.

The English Presbyterian Mission is doing a very fine work in this part of China, Amoy and Swatow being the controlling centres. 'The native Church,' the report says, 'gives us a leverage which, by the power of the Spirit of God, is producing great results, and which must in the future produce still greater.' The Amoy Mission has of late years developed in the most encouraging way. There are eight organized and thirty-nine not yet organized congregations, with 1006 communicants ; while at Swatow there are nine organized congregations and eighteen not yet organized, and 1100 Church members. Thirty years ago there were only three communicants ; now a native Church with twenty-seven congregations, 2000 persons under its charge ; a native moderator, Rev. Lim Huang ; native contributions amounting to 1897 dollars ; and the Church has started its own Missionary Association, and has chosen the island of Namoa as its first field. This mission also maintains a large printing establishment and good educational work ; which and the women's work, under the care of Miss Ricketts, is very valuable. One very interesting fact was mentioned by Dr. Lyall—that a Chinese merchant (not Christian, I believe) had offered 2000 dollars to help in establishing a women's hospital.

After making these pleasant calls on the coast, we drew near to Hong-Kong. This island is a Crown colony, ceded by the Chinese Government in 1841. It is eleven miles long by from two to five miles broad, and twenty-seven miles in circumference. It consists of a broken ridge of lofty hills, with but little ground which admits of cultivation, not one-twentieth part of the surface being available for agricultural uses. The harbour has an area of ten square miles, and divides the island from the mainland. It is shut in with lofty hills, set as it were in a frame of the most diversified and picturesque scenery. Victoria itself far exceeds as a city anything which is to be seen elsewhere in China. The city is well built, and the streets are broad and well kept. There is both gas and electric illumination, a well-ordered police force, many important and some imposing-looking buildings, public and private. The Hong-Kong and Shanghai Bank occupies finer premises than any bank in London. The hills rising almost immediately from the harbour, the city spreads along the shore, and some of the streets which climb the hillside are so steep that no wheeled carriage can be used on them, and they are broken at short distances by flights of steps. Jinrickshas are used in great numbers on the more level roads. To ascend the Peak the only available conveyance is the chair, carried by coolies.

During our stay in this city, Dr. Glover was the guest of Mr. Bonfield, the minister of the Union Church, while I was entertained by Dr. Chalmers, one of the oldest representatives of the London Mission in China. We saw as much as our time would allow of the work of the London Mission, the Basle and Berlin Missions, and the Church Missionary Society. The Sunday we spent in Hong-Kong was fully occupied, Dr. Glover and I taking the services at Union Church morning and evening, and in the afternoon we addressed a large gathering of Chinese Christians in one of the chapels of the London Missionary Society. While we were glad that the time of our return, and the prospect of meeting with our friends at home, was drawing near, I think we both had a feeling of regret that after that service we should have no further opportunity of meeting with Chinese Christians, with whom in different parts of this great empire we have had such frequent and pleasant intercourse.

While at Hong-Kong we availed ourselves of the opportunity of paying a visit to Canton, probably the largest and certainly the most picturesque and characteristic city in China. We made the journey up the river Pearl in a very fine English-built boat called the Fat-Shan, of immense beam for her length, small draught, and burden of 2000 tons. There were only four or five European travellers, and for these excellent accommodation was provided. There was a larger number of Chinese intermediate passengers, and a very large number of third-class Chinese passengers, who are carried at a low rate. As it can never be known but by the event who are the passengers thus carried, every possible care is taken to prevent what is now happily of rare occurrence, the piratical seizure of the vessel. They are all stowed away on the lower deck, and over each communication with the upper deck a heavy iron grating is fastened, not to be removed till the vessel reaches its destination, and at each of these a well-armed foreigner keeps guard, while in the saloon is a stand of arms—rifles and bayonets—ready for use, should they be needed for self-protection.

Approaching Canton by river, two things impress the traveller—the size of the city and suburbs, which spread along the river for some miles, and the enormous boat-population. The sides of this wide river and the adjacent creeks are simply crowded with boats of different kinds—junks, sampans, slipper-boats—many ranks deep, and in these people are born, marry, bring up families, and die. It is supposed that the boat-population numbers a quarter of a million.

The population of the city and suburbs is put down at 1,600,000. Chinese statistics, however, must always be taken with some measure of reserve. Many of the boats which are moored by the river-side are fixtures, and are used as places of entertainment and refreshment. They are known as flower-boats, and many of them are places of very questionable reputation. The boats which ply for hire are, to a large extent, worked by women, who are strong and healthy-looking, and skilful in the exercise of their calling. It is a very common sight to see a woman standing at the oar, which she vigorously plies, while her baby is slung at her back. We were taken up the river some miles by a woman known as 'Susan,' recommended to us by the captain as quite trustworthy—the mother of seven children ; five of them were on board, and the mother and eldest daughter worked the boat, and did it well.

The native city of Canton is about two miles in breadth and ten miles in circumference, the enclosing wall being broad and high. There is a partition wall running east and west, dividing the city into two unequal parts. The suburbs are large and important, stretching along the river for nearly five miles. What is now called the new city was formerly known as the southern suburbs. Looking over the city from any elevated spot, the general appearance is like that of all Chinese cities we have seen, flat and monotonous, the watch-towers on the walls, two pagodas, and some large structures belonging to pawnbrokers, and the Roman Catholic cathedral, being almost the only noticeable elevations. The two great features of interest in Canton are the enormous boat-population, of which much might be said, and the business streets, which unquestionably have a character of their own, and a character so peculiar and complex as to render description impossible. They are more narrow, more crowded, more busy, and make a richer display than any streets we have seen in China. The widest street is not more than twelve feet in breadth, the narrowest not more than seven or eight feet. The shops on either side are, according to Chinese custom, open to the streets, the entire front being removed when business begins, and in these you not only see salesmen ready to dispose of manufactured goods, but artisans, most of them half naked, busily engaged in their manufacture. These narrow streets are invaded by shopkeepers in such a way as to render them practically much narrower, and from every shop there projects at least one lacquered tablet, with gilded legend or device, while every piece of vacant ground is taken possession of by itinerant tradesmen. These narrow streets are so thronged that it is a matter of great difficulty to make your way through them, and you are continually obliged to turn aside—so far as an aside is possible—and make way for a string of blind beggars, or coolies with their burdens swinging from their bamboo shoulder-poles, or for some sedan chair which is forcing its way along. The strangely dressed and still more strangely undressed people, the wonderful exhibitions in the shops, the gleaming tablets, the rush of vigorous and noisy life, is exhilarating, fascinating, bewildering, and, as you find after a few hours' experience, very exhausting. The streets did not strike me as exceptionally dirty ; they are paved with transverse slabs of stone, not closely joined, and beneath flows or stagnates the drain. This arrangement has the advantage that the pavement can easily be kept comparatively clean, and the disadvantage of allowing the disgusting odours which rise from the festering filth beneath to assail the nose of every passer-by.

We saw a little of the work of the Wesleyan Mission and of the American Presbyterian, finding here as elsewhere that the most encouraging work was done, not in the city itself, but, working from the city as a centre, in the country for many miles round about. A good work is also doing at Fat-Shan, especially in connection with the hospital, which accomodates fifty patients. Last year 3000 in and out patients were treated, and two hundred operations performed. The popular appreciation of the work done may be gathered from the fact that during the past year more than 2000 dollars were received in fees. Canton is interesting to all who are interested in Chinese missions as being the place to which the first Protestant missionary (the Rev. Robert Morrison, of the London Missionary Society) was sent. He arrived there in September, 1807, and he died in Canton in 1834. What a wonderful change has been wrought since 1807, and even since 1834!

We went back to Hong-Kong by the Fat-Shan, to spend one more day there, and then left China, and the many friends who have rendered our visit so pleasant, for our homeward journey on April 30, 1891.

CHAPTER XIII.

THE RELIGIONS OF CHINA.

Chinamen blend all religions—Conduct of the Viceroy of Shansi—Ancestral worship—Chief features of this worship—The ancestral tablet—Significance of the worship—It is a great hindrance to Christianity—Confucianism—Taouism—Buddhism.

ONE cannot be long in China without feeling how difficult it is to understand the religions which prevail there, and to determine with any approach to accuracy the religious position of the ordinary Chinaman. The difficulty results from the fact that there are several distinct, or at least distinguishable systems, not only existing side by side as separate and rival religions, but often blended together in the most remarkable and confusing manner. Confucianism is universally prevalent, and the rites of ancestral worship, with sundry modifications, are universally maintained ; but with these there will be very often mixed up, and not infrequently in a very grotesque way, some recognition of the claims and pretensions of Buddhism or Taouism, or both. A Chinaman thinks it wise and prudent, without committing himself too deeply to any one of these systems, to keep on reasonably good terms with all. The various religious observances in which he from time to time takes part do not involve a very large expenditure of either time or money, and may possibly, he thinks, in some unthought-of way, bring to him some good, or avert from him some evil, in this world or the next.

And it is not only the poor and ignorant who exhibit this strange blending of different religions without any apparent sense of inconsistency. It is seen in all classes, from the highest to the lowest. In the drought which threatened the crops in the spring of the year 1891 in Shansi, the provincial governor was unceasing in his attempts to move Heaven to send down rain. He visited in person the most noted temples in the district. At the famous well at Ching-Tzu he sacrificed ; he sent a deputy to a miraculous well in Chihli ; he consulted magicians and sorcerers ; and, that he might leave no means untried, went to the Roman Catholic cathedral, and took part in the recital of the prayers.

In a long and interesting conversation we had with Lo-Fung-lu, private secretary to Li-Hung-Chang, we asked him how he would characterize the great religions of China. He replied that it was exceedingly difficult to give anything like a definition, as these systems ran into one another to so large an extent, and were accepted by different people with so many modifications. But, speaking generally, he should be inclined to describe Confucianism as Atheistic, Buddhism as Pantheistic, and Taouism as Materialistic ; 'but,' he added, with a smile, 'you do not define a Chinaman's religious position when you give him a name and call him a Confucianist, a Buddhist, or a Taouist; he may be that, but he is usually something more.'

ANCESTRAL WORSHIP.

Ancestral worship may be regarded as the indigenous and universal religion of China. Confucianism, Taouism, and Buddhism, are commonly spoken of as the three great religions of the empire, and correctly enough; but at the back of all these, and linked more or less closely with all of them, is the wonderful system of ancestral worship, which has a stronger hold upon China than anything else. Many suppose, from passages discovered in the most ancient Chinese records, that the earliest form of Chinese religion was monotheistic. At a very early period, however, this simple primitive religion became associated with the worship of deceased ancestors, and spirits supposed to preside over the different operations of Nature. Long prior to the time of Confucius, there was widely, if not universally, prevalent the custom of sacrificing to, and worshipping the shades of, departed ancestors; and it formed a part, and a very important part, of that original system of religion into which both Confucianism and Taouism have struck their roots.

This, the oldest form of worship, is also the most universal. In every Chinese home, at every Chinese tomb, this worship is maintained. This form of religion comes home to the Chinese mind, we might almost say to the Chinese heart, as nothing else does.

There is a Chinese saying which has acquired proverbial currency, ' The idols belong to everybody, but our ancestors are our own.'

Dr. Blodget, of Peking, in his paper on Ancestral Worship, tells us that in the *Shu King*, the earliest authentic history of China, the work which was edited by Confucius, there are no fewer than twenty-one allusions to ancestral worship ; and from a careful study of these notices he draws these conclusions among others : That ancestral worship was practised in the very dawn of Chinese history ; that even in those early days it was not a mere local usage, but a well-established religious cult, and a prominent and very important part of the state religion ; that offerings of various kinds were made in the ancestral temples ; that the deceased ancestors were regarded as having a real existence, and as being able to receive prayers and offerings, and also to participate actively in human affairs ; that the deceased emperors were very early, if not from the first, elevated in rank so as to be associated with Shang-te, or heaven, and with earth at the suburban sacrifices at the summer and winter solstices. In fact, all the essential features of ancestral worship as maintained to-day are set forth, with sundry modifications, in that old-world record. And this singular form of worship, lasting on through ages and generations, enters into and most closely affects the life of China. In all parts of the empire, in all classes of society, its influence is felt. Rich and poor, learned and ignorant, prince and peasant, are alike subject to its sway.

Originating, as it probably did, in a distorted view of filial piety, we are reminded by those who are inclined to speak tenderly of this superstition, that there is a certain element of truth embedded in it, and that intelligent Chinese declare that what we speak of as ancestral worship is not, in their case at least, idolatrous, and, indeed, is not in any proper sense to be regarded as worship at all. It is only reasonable to suppose that while the practice of ancestral worship is universal, many different opinions are entertained concerning the rites which are so generally observed. The question, however, is not, What is the view taken of the practice by a select few? but, What is the view taken by the mass and multitude of the Chinese people?

The use of the ancestral tablet is now universal, and there can be little doubt that idolatrous worship is paid to it. To quote from Dr. Blodget, 'The tablet consists of two small, upright pieces of wood, fitted to each other and placed on a wooden pedestal. These pieces of wood present two outward and two inner surfaces. The writing is upon the front outer surface and the front inner surface. This latter has written upon it the dates of the birth and death of the deceased, his surname, name and title, with the additional characters which have been rendered *Shêu chu,* "the lodging-place of his spirit," or "the place in which his spirit bears rule or exercises lordship." This inscription relates especially to the family.

'The former, that is, the front surface, has an inscription which bears some relation to the Government, and states both the age of the deceased, and what honours he may have received or hoped for, and ending with the words *Shêu wei*, "the seat or throne of his spirit."

'These two inscriptions, when first written, are both incomplete. The point or dot upon the *chu* on the inside surface, and that upon the *wei* on the outside surface, are both omitted. To impose these dots upon these two characters is the great ceremony in consecrating the tablet, which is thus vivified and made an object of worship. The usual time for this ceremony is the day before the burial of the dead.

'In writing the first and incomplete inscription on the tablet, it is common to seek for a member of the national academy, or, among the common people, a literary graduate of the second degree, thereby as it were giving to the writing the imperial sanction. After this, to perform the important act of dotting the tablet, a mandarin of higher grade is invited to be present, or, in the case of the common people, a literary graduate. He comes invested with the authority of the emperor, who, as the son of Heaven, and bearing rule by the decree of Heaven, is at the head of the national cult, and directs what gods are and what gods are not to be worshipped, and deifies and appoints to their place those whom he judges worthy of this honour. Thus, in a small way, which bears some resemblance to the appointment of national gods, the ancestors of the people are also made gods, objects of worship, and enthroned in each household.

'Along with this chief personage, four other mandarins of lesser grade are invited to be present and assist in the ceremony. . . . The red dots are now imposed by the chief mandarin.   These red dots are then covered with dots of black ink by the same person and with the same ceremonies.   The consecration of the tablet being now finished, it is returned to its casket, which is then closed.

'The chief mourner, after this, takes the tablet from one of the attendant magistrates in both hands, in a very reverential manner, and sets it upright upon a small table in front of the coffin.   The magistrate who has imposed the dots then comes forward with his four associates, and while all are kneeling on a mat before the tablet, pours out three chalices of wine as a libation, after which the five prostrate themselves three times before the tablet, bringing the head each time to the ground.   Then all retire, their duty being accomplished.

'The tablet thus consecrated is carried out the next day to the cemetery, on a pavilion adorned with hangings of silk, its place in the funeral procession being some distance in front of the catafalque.   At evening it is returned to the home of the eldest son, where incense is burned before it morning and evening, and the customary offerings are made during the three years of mourning.   When these are finished, the tablet is transferred to the ancestral hall, to be worshipped with the other tablets of the clan, with the customary libations and offerings, on the days set apart for such service.

'Such is the ancestral tablet in its consecration and uses.   Among the common people there is less ceremony and expenditure of money, while the rich and those high in rank lavish their wealth on this and all that pertains to funeral rites. The customs above described vary in different parts of the country, but the essential things are the same. There is a kind of incorporation of the spirit in the tablet as its visible home, where it receives offerings and prayers, and manifests its good will or disapprobation. This is implied throughout in the preparation and uses of the tablet.'

Dr. Blodget, whose description of the ancestral tablet I have now given, freely admits that those who practise these rites may differ widely in intent, and he distributes the Chinese who worship their deceased ancestors into four classes :

First.—Those who do this in the belief that their ancestors still exist, that they have power for good or evil over their descendants, and that they may be appeased by offerings, or offended by the withholding of them.

Second.—Those who are agnostic in regard to these points, who not only do not profess to know, but who think that nothing can be known in regard to deceased ancestors and their relations to the living. If such persons be asked why they sacrifice to the dead, they will reply that they do this to manifest their filial piety.

Third.—Those who deny the continued existence of their deceased ancestors and all objective reality in their worship. Their reason for maintaining such worship would be the same as that just mentioned.

Fourth.—The fourth and by far the largest class is composed of those who worship their ancestors, without inquiry or thought as to the reasonableness

O

of such worship, simply because it is the national and hereditary custom.

These four classes would all hold themselves bound to act in accordance with the rule of Confucius, 'Sacrifice (to departed ancestors) as though they were present;' 'Sacrifice (to the gods or spirits) as though they were present.' Confucius has so worded this rule for worship that all may follow it, whatever their belief or want of belief. He is silent as to the existence or non-existence of the dead.

The question as to the way in which ancestral worship should be regarded and dealt with by Christian missionaries is a live question in China to-day, and it is a very important question. Much depends on the answer that is given to it. No subject was more keenly discussed at the recent Shanghai Conference, and no discussion was followed with greater interest by the outside public. The two sides of the question were looked at, but the almost universal feeling was that nothing in the shape of compromise could be even seriously thought of.

Dr. Martin, who 'urges a plea for toleration,' begins his paper with an admission which cuts the ground away from under his own feet. 'If,' he says, 'I were called on to name the most serious impediment to the conversion of the Chinese, I should without hesitation point to the worship of ancestors. Gathering into itself all that is deemed most sacred in family or state, it rises before us like a mountain barrier, hoary with age and buttressed on the bed-rock of the empire.'

In estimating the character of ancestral worship as

practised at present by the Chinese, it is a fact too significant to be overlooked that Chinese converts are unanimous and emphatic in their condemnation of it. From those who have been delivered from the thrall of this superstition, and who know what it means, no plea for toleration proceeds. In their judgment the practice is utterly wrong, and obviously inconsistent with the fundamental principles of the Christian religion, and they regard with feelings of almost incredulous astonishment the action of those who try to prove that it is not idolatrous. The Rev. Y. K. Yen, a native Episcopal clergyman, whom I had the pleasure of meeting at Shanghai, entertains and does not hesitate to express the strongest opinions on this point, as a few words from his address at the Shanghai Conference will show. 'The belief,' he says, 'is an idolatrous belief, and the worship is an idolatrous worship. . . . The two ideas of paying human honours and divine honours to ancestors are so combined that we cannot separate them. It is quite true that among the educated there are those who disown the divine element in the worship, and claim that they reverence them as human beings ; but they are a very small class indeed. Even as regards these—whatever they may say in theory—I cannot help believing that they still have an idea that ancestors either watch over them and protect them, or have it in their power to do them harm. . . . I think that every missionary ought to tell the Chinese to reverence their ancestors, but at the same time let it be without those forms that are current among them. . . . Often when preaching in the chapel the Chinese would come to me and say, "You do not worship your ancestors." I reply, "I do honour them, but as men, and not as God," and they are quite satisfied. . . . Christianity gives all the human heart needs, and the man who teaches it, and he who sincerely accepts it, will understand it poorly if he still thinks that ancestral worship must be retained to supplement it.' These words, coming from one who is a Chinaman and a Christian, have great weight.

CONFUCIANISM.

Confucianism is the state religion of China, and every Chinaman is more or less a follower of Confucius. Strictly speaking, however, Confucianism is rather a system of morality than a system of religion. It is wonderful how large a place Confucius still holds in China, and how powerful and widespread an influence he still exerts.

Koong-foo-tsze—or Confucius, as the Jesuits determined to call him—lived in the sixth century before Christ. With his strong conservative instincts and profound respect for antiquity, he accepted without question or controversy the religion that he found already existing in China; and in his teaching he looked at man merely as an occupant of this world, and dealt exclusively with those relations which the individual man sustains to his neighbours and to the state. Whatever may have been the personal belief of Confucius, it is admitted that he has very little to say about God, or those relations which subsist between God and man, and, according to the best authorities, he has very little or nothing to say about immortality and the unseen world. Confucius keeps clear of all speculative questions ; his teaching is intensely practical. His position is substantially that of the secularist—the agnostic. Man, he thinks, has enough to occupy him in dealing with the present life—in ascertaining and determining what he shall do and what he shall abstain from doing here, in the discharge of duty, the cultivation of virtue.

Confucius does not pronounce judgment on the things that are beyond ; he simply refuses to discuss them—to take them into practical account. He finds a system of religion existing, and he leaves it where he finds it ; and he builds up a good system of morals, which is to a large extent independent of religious sanctions. In his teaching Confucius gave great prominence to the doctrine of filial piety, and, finding ancestral worship already existing, may be said to have re-established it on a broader and surer basis, buttressing it with moral sanctions, so that it has become the one religion, in the observances of which all the Chinese people unite. And yet, in dealing with ancestral worship, he is careful not to commit himself by the expression of any definite belief as to the continued existence of the dead or their relations to the living.

'On this point he does not encourage inquiry. His language is, " While you do not know about life, how can you know about death ? " " If I were to say the dead have knowledge of what takes place, I fear lest filial sons and dutiful grandsons would neglect the living to serve the dead ; if I were to say that the dead have no knowledge of what takes place, I am afraid lest unfilial sons would leave their parents unburied. You need not wish to know whether the dead have knowledge or not. There is no present urgency about the point. Hereafter you will know for yourself." In such ignorance as regards the future he lived himself, and in such ignorance he left his followers.'

There are great differences of opinion among competent Chinese scholars as to the views entertained by Confucianists as to the being and worship of God, and whether, when they speak of worshipping Heaven, they have any idea of a supreme, invisible, and personal Ruler of the universe. It is a question difficult to determine. The great majority of those with whom I conversed upon this subject in China had the impression that when the Chinese talk of adoring heaven and earth, they have no idea of a personal God, but are worshipping and serving the creature rather than the Creator.

While in Shansi we had a long and very interesting conversation with a Chinese gentleman, to whom our missionary friend had rendered important medical service. He was a pronounced Confucianist, a literary graduate of some standing. Among other things we spoke to him about God and God's love, and asked him whether he believed that God loves us. Upon which he rose from his seat, and in apparently eloquent terms, certainly with much apparent earnestness and many gesticulations, he told us what his creed was. 'Of course,' he said, ' God loves us. Heaven is our Father, and Earth is our Mother. Here is Heaven overarching us all, and we are, whether we think of it or not, always in the embrace of our Father; and here is Earth stretching out everywhere underneath us, and, whether we think of it or not, we are always resting on the bosom of our Mother.' But so far as I could gather his meaning as given us by our interpreter, he was, when speaking of heaven and earth, thinking of two divinities, and not of that one God who is both in heaven above and on earth beneath, making Himself known by the things that He has made. At the close of the conversation he reminded us with Confucian self-complacency that his religion was good enough for him. ' It teaches us,' he said, ' the proprieties, and it will be well with us now and always if we but observe them.'

A great deal is said about the Chinese system of morals, and there can be no doubt that it is a very remarkable one, and such as can be found nowhere else apart from the teaching of Christianity. From the most remote antiquity a number of very admirable maxims and proverbs have been handed down, and China's greatest sage—Confucius—has formulated a system of morals which is confessedly one of great beauty and worth, and which, however little carried out in practice, is in China to-day theoretically held in very high esteem.

Dr. Edkins—one of our most reliable authorities on all such questions—says, ' What is the Confucian morality on which such high encomiums have been passed? A follower of that sage would probably reply to this question by referring to the San-Kang-woo-chang, " the three relations, and the five constant virtues." The three relations, to which belong corresponding duties, are those of prince and subject, father and son, and husband and wife ; the five virtues, whose obligation is constant and universal, are benevolence, uprightness, politeness, knowledge, and faithfulness. Politeness includes, in the Chinese meaning of the word, compliance with all social and public customs transmitted by wise men and good kings. The native term for knowledge means rather the prudence gained by knowledge. The word for faithfulness means both to be trustworthy and also to trust to, and refers chiefly to friendship.'

Virtue is defined as consisting in following our nature, and vice as deviating from it.

And 'what,' says Dr. Edkins, 'has the result been on the Chinese of the Confucian morality? It has not made them a moral people. Many of the social virtues are extensively practised among them, but they exhibit to the observer a lamentable want of moral strength. Commercial integrity and speaking the truth are far less common among them than in Christian countries. The standard of principle among them is kept low by the habits of the people. They do not appear to feel ashamed when the discovery is made that they have told an untruth. Falsehood is too often a favourite weapon of the diplomacy in social life. There is a palpable lack of sensitiveness on this and other points which indicates the want of honourable principle in the national character. This renders the nation feeble in war, and open to new temptations—such as, for example, the use of opium. Another cause of moral weakness among the Chinese is the practice of polygamy, an institution which operates as mischievously on them as on other Oriental nations. The state of opinion is such in that country, that in some cases the taking of a second wife during the lifetime of the first is regarded as a virtue. It is, for instance, the duty of a filial son to marry again if he is without children by his first wife, in order to have sons who may continue the sacrifices at the ancestral tomb. The chief evil attending domestic slavery in China is, that it directly promotes concubinage to a vast extent. Thus the Confucian morality, though good in theory, has not been successful in bringing the nation to a good moral condition.'

Confucianism, if you do not look beyond the teaching of Confucius, can scarcely be called a religion. There is as to everything above or beyond this life a well-satisfied confession of ignorance, a self-complacent agnosticism. All these deeper questions are put on one side, as those which can afford to wait, so that matters of greater urgency pertaining to this life may receive due attention.

It is a singular thing that while Confucius did not impress upon his followers very strongly the importance of any kind of worship, he himself throughout the empire has become an object of worship. 'A year after Confucius was dead, a funeral temple was erected to his honour. His disciple, Tsze-Kung, stayed for six years at his tomb. In his temple were buried articles of dress that he had worn, with his musical instruments and books. Sacrifices were directed by royal authority to be offered to him. It was not till many years after that, an emperor of the

Han dynasty passing the spot, a bullock was slain, to be presented to him as a sacrifice. It is now universal to offer a bullock with other animals to Confucius in every Chinese city. No priests are employed. It is an official act, forming a part of the annual duties of the city magistrate and other resident officers.'

TAOUISM.

Taouism lays claim to an antiquity equal to that of Confucianism. Lao-tsze, the founder of this religion, was born, it is commonly supposed, about fifty years before Confucius, and must, therefore, have been an old man when China's great sage began to claim the attention of his countrymen. Of the personal history of Lao-tsze no historical record has been preserved ; but, as is so often the case, where history fails legend sets itself to supply the deficiency, and China is full of marvellous tales of the birth and career of the old philosopher. According to one legend, he was born an old man eighty years of age, and was called Lao-tsu, the 'old boy,' or Lau-Kinu, the 'venerable prince.' It seems generally agreed that he was 'keeper of the archives,' or 'keeper of the treasury,' in the imperial court of Chow, and that at least on one occasion Confucius had an interview with him, and soon after this Lao-tsze resigned his office, and in retirement from the world gave himself up to the cultivation of *Taou* (the way) and *Tĭh* (virtue).

It is exceedingly difficult to determine the exact position occupied by Lao-tsze as a religious and philosophical teacher. 'In the *Taou-tĭh-King*,' says

Professor Douglas, ' Laou-tsze has elaborated his ideal of the relations existing between the universe and that which he calls *Taou*. The primary meaning of this name of a thing which he declares to be " without name," is " the way." Hence it has acquired the symbolical meanings of " the right course of conduct," " reason," and it also signifies " the Word " (Logos). By all these meanings it has been severally rendered by the translators of Laou-tsze's celebrated work. . . . If we were compelled to adopt a single word to represent the *Taou* of Laou-tsze, we should prefer the sense in which it is used by Confucius, " the way," that is, μέθοδος. " If I were endowed with prudence I should walk in the great *Taou*. . . .The great *Taou* is exceeding plain, but the people like the footpaths," said Laou-tsze. But it is more than the way. It is the way and the way-goer. It is an eternal road ; along it all beings and things walk ; but no being made it, for it is a being itself; it is everything and nothing, and the cause and effect of all. All things originate from *Taou*, conform to *Taou*, and to *Taou* at last they return.'

There is no doubt that Lao-tsze was a great and original teacher, and many of his wise and profound utterances deserve to be held in remembrance. According to the most competent scholars, he knew nothing of a personal God ; indeed, his system, so far as it can be understood, seems exclusive of any such idea. The gross superstitions and magical arts of modern Taouism cannot find a sanction, or even the slightest encouragement, in any recorded word of Lao-tsze himself.

In considering the religions of China, however, we must take Taouism as we find it to-day, and that is altogether distinct from the system which is expounded in the *Taou-tĭh-King*. The old mystical and transcendental philosophy and religion of Lao-tsze has been displaced by charms and magical arts and incantations, by means of which the Taouist priests impose on an ignorant and superstitious people. In the metaphysical and speculative system of Laou-tsze there was no room for an imposing array of gods and goddesses ; but when Buddhism invaded China, 'not to be outdone by their rivals the Buddhists, who could point to Shâkyamuni as deity incarnate, the Taouist priests deified Laou-tsze ; and the two sects rivalled each other in providing gods of every kind for the wants of the people. Whenever popular sentiment seemed to indicate that it was ripe for such a step, a new god was provided, either by the deification of a hero, or the personification of a principle or social element, such as wealth, war, and longevity.'

In a sketch of this kind no attempt can be made to describe the Taouist mythology, or its superstitious rites and ceremonies, upon payment for the performance of which the Taouist priests chiefly depend for their livelihood. The Taouist priests are very numerous, and may be easily recognized by their dress. You meet with them everywhere. They are an ignorant set of men, often of questionable character, and even of unquestionably bad character.

According to Professor Douglas, 'by the educated classes they are looked down upon with supreme contempt, and only such of their beliefs as have received the approval of the government at different times, for various causes, are in any way recognized by any but the most ignorant of the people. By law, candidates for the priesthood should go through a course of study extending over five years, at the end of which time they take the vows, and receive a licence from the local mandarins. But practically their novitiate is spent in serving the priests, who impart to them only such knowledge of chicanery and fraud as they themselves possess, and a smattering of ethical science, to enable them to prompt the oracular responses of the gods to the inquiries of the sick and dying. The social morality of the priests is of the most degraded kind, and the nunneries, which, in imitation of the Buddhists, they have established throughout the empire, are by common report described as the haunts of every vice. Without a belief in any god apart from deified men, without the purer motives which influence the Buddhists in their endeavour to reach a higher life, having drifted, century after century, further and further away from all that is noble, unselfish, and true, the modern Taouists have sunk lower in the estimation of their fellow-men than any but the most degraded of idolaters.'

BUDDHISM.

Buddhism was brought into China from India in the first century, or rather, perhaps, it should be said that it then first struck its roots into Chinese soil and life. That time may be regarded as marking the commencement of that vigorous growth which made it one of the great religions of China. It is said that so early as the year 250 B.C. Buddhist missionaries found their way into China. But Buddhism as a religious system cannot be said to have effected a real lodgment in the land until it was officially recognized by the Emperor Mingti of the Han dynasty. It is said that in the year 61 A.D. this emperor had a dream which very powerfully impressed him ; he saw a foreign god entering his palace, and he was led to regard this dream as affording him a divine intimation that he should introduce the Buddhist religion to the land over which he ruled. Thereupon he despatched ambassadors to India, who were instructed to make all needful inquiries, and who on their return brought back with them an image of Buddha and a number of priests.

These were received with much favour by the emperor, and, sustained by the influence of the imperial court, they set to work to make known the principles of Buddhism, and to urge its claims. This, we are told, they did with so much success, that in a comparatively short time Buddhist temples and priests were to be seen in almost every part of the empire. This system, however, did not uninterruptedly enjoy the favour of the court, and its adherents had on several occasions to endure severe persecution ; but the opposition it had to encounter failed to check its growth, and, according to a census taken at the end of the thirteenth century, there were in China at that time 42,318 Buddhist temples and 213,148 priests.

In China Buddha is worshipped in the form of a triune deity, and the three persons in the Buddhist trinity are known as Buddha Past, Buddha Present, and Buddha Future. As we have seen in the case of Taouism, so Buddhism soon developed into a complicated system of idolatry, Buddha himself being the central object of worship.

To quote from Archdeacon Moule, 'In a country like China, so practical, so positive, so materialistic, it is difficult to distinguish between Buddhist orthodox observances, and such apocryphal superstitious glosses as the character and condition of the people have evolved. The goal of the consistent and orthodox Buddhist is Nirvâna ; and Nirvâna, according to orthodox interpretation, is "the great deathless state, which is tranquil, and free from birth, decay, sickness, grief, and joy. The word Nirvâna means originally the state of a blown-out flame. The three-tongued fire thus extinguished consists of lust, ill-will, and delusion ; and the blowing out of the flame means a total cessation of all evil passions, and all desires for good and bad alike ; especially the desire for individual and conscious existence." "Nirvâna is a state neither of consciousness nor of unconsciousness ; individuality is gone, and the desire for life is an ignorant blunder." "A higher state remains, that of Pari Nirvâna, where complete extinction is obtained of all the elements or seeds of bodily existence." It seems that not merely the northern Buddhists of China, Thibet, and Japan, but even the more orthodox southern Buddhists in Ceylon, Burmah, and Siam, decline to accept this doctrine of practical annihilation. And later Buddhism, constrained by this revolt, has elaborated a system of twenty-six tiers of heavens ; the lower levels being full of light, purity, and placid contemplation, and thus lying more within the reach of immortal but conscious spirits ; and the higher soaring stages are ignored by popular Buddhism. The doctrine of the Paradise of the Far West is directly connected with Amidâbha Buddha. . . . Now in China every Buddhist monk or nun, and every devout worshipper, repeats morning, noon, and night the name of Amidâbha, as *the* great charm against evil—*the* sure way of access to the heaven of light where Amidâbha sits in glory, discoursing on religion.

'" Good morning," says a priest. " Amidâbha " (*o mee do fuh*). " Have you had your rice ? Amidâbha." " What is your honourable age ? Amidâbha." " It looks like rain. Amidâbha." " I have a severe headache ! Amidâbha." " If you wish to reach the city quickly, take the first turn to the right and the second to the left. Amidâbha." " Farewell. Amidâbha ; " and (*aside*), " What a queer fellow, that foreigner ! Amidâbha."

' This special Buddha, and his western land of bliss and of beauty, . . . this is popular Buddhism ; this forms one great dream of heaven for many Buddhists. Yet even this reformed and reconstructed Buddhism does not satisfy the practical Chinese. Their souls, cleaving to the dust of demand and supply of this mortal life, scatter thick dust from their wings when they rise to the contemplation of another life, and make heaven itself earthly, avaricious, profane. And to a Buddhist merchant or tradesman, the idea of modern, popular Buddhism, to the effect that heaven is only earth over again, with more money and more luxury, must be specially attractive and sympathetic. His chief object of worship is the god of wealth, represented either by a paper inscription or an image ; and the idea of heaven being the acquisition of more money in the spirit-world, the practical nature of the Chinese leads them to make preparations for this happy consummation while still below. And here is the opportunity for the priests. . . . The priests of certain temples in the neighbourhood especially of Ningpo have a kind of monopoly of the sale of paper money for the use of the dead in the spirit-world. These "spiritual notes" are sold at almost every temple, but they are specially valuable at certain places, called the Lin-Fung shrines ; and on the day when the birthday of the deified hero of the shrine is observed. They are sold singly or in bundles. A single note would cost about three halfpence ; and for the devout and consistent Buddhist it will be cashed in the spirit-world for about one thousand times the original cost. In order to become available for the use of the soul, the notes must be spiritualized by burning ; and the fortune for another world of a Buddhist devotee, consisting of chests filled with these flimsy papers, will be solemnly burnt after death, and be thus wafted into the unseen. Imitation dollars made of paste-board and covered over with thin foil, and paper

P

imitations of silver ingots, are also purchaseable in the shops, and are guaranteed by the priests as a sure medium of transferring money for the use of the souls in the other world.'

The Chinese Buddhism of to-day is a complex system of idolatry, under which the most gross kinds of superstition shelter themselves.

The priesthood is supplied chiefly from the poorer classes of society. The Buddhist priests whom we met were of a very low type. So far as we could learn, they are held in very little esteem by their fellow-countrymen. They are an uneducated class, having little knowledge of their own religion and little interest in it save as a means of livelihood. Many of them are men of bad moral character, and confirmed opium-smokers. The priests chiefly reside in monasteries, though many of them travel about the country, in some districts in companies, in other districts singly. There are not many Chinese who have a good word to speak about the Buddhist priesthood, and the Buddhist nunneries have not a much better character than the Taouist.

In Thibet, Mongolia, Manchuria, and some parts of North China, there prevails a form of Buddhism known as Lamaism, the Grand Lama of Thibet being acknowledged as the spiritual head, to whom all the lamas or priests own subjection. The grand lama is the political as well as religious ruler of Thibet, though acknowledging the suzerainty of the Emperor of China. Like the Buddhist priests, the lamas are celibates, and are recognized by their shaven heads and yellow robes. They usually reside in monasteries, and there are some large lama monasteries in Peking and other places in North China. Prayer-wheels are often placed at the gates of their temples. ' On each wheel a prayer is recorded, and the votary who is passing by, or who is unable to remain in the temple till the service is concluded, repeats once the prayer that he is about to set in motion, and then turns the wheel and goes his way. The wheel is supposed to waft the prayer to heaven, and the petition is considered to be repeated as often as it revolves.' Woo-tai-shan, in Shansi, is a great centre of Lamaism, to which large numbers of pilgrims flock. Dr. Edkins, who has given a very interesting account of a visit he paid to Woo-tai-shan, tells us that at that time there were 1000 Mongol lamas and 2000 Chinese lamas and Hooshangs resident there. It is said that many of the ceremonies of Lamaism have been borrowed from the Roman Catholic Church. However that may be, it is generally admitted that there are some very remarkable points of resemblance, which cannot be overlooked by any one who compares the ceremonial of Roman Catholicism with that of Buddhism as it prevails in Thibet.

With the existence of all these different forms of religion, the one thing that impressed me while in China, more than almost anything else, was the apparent absence of deep and real religious sentiment. In Japan we found temples well kept and well frequented. In China, temples of all kinds are ill kept, and, except on certain days, without worshippers. There is the worship of idols ; but the Chinese almost without exception seem to feel that there is not much in it. Certain religious ceremonies are observed, and the observance is reckoned among the proprieties of life ; but there is no outward indication that any of the deeper feelings of the heart are stirred by the transaction. In China the gods are either ' respectfully neglected or ceremonially worshipped.' The advice of Confucius was to ' reverence the gods, but to keep at a distance from them '—advice which is very generally accepted and acted on. The ordinary Chinaman is practically if not professedly a secularist, an agnostic, with certain superstitions, idolatrous additions which are accepted and observed out of a prudential regard for self, or a politic consideration of others. There has been a great deal of talk about agnosticism in our own country of late years. Well, it should be remembered that agnosticism is not a new thing; it has been tried on a grand scale in China for 2500 years, and the miserable result of that experiment you may see in China to-day. The moral conscience of the people has not been so much perverted as paralyzed. It has been well said that the two great wants of China are character and conscience. And China's needs can be only met in one way. Western education, Western civilization, Western arts and sciences, railways, telegraphs, telephones, steel-clad war-vessels and arms of precision, whatever else they may do, will never give to any people character and conscience. China's great need can only be met by the Gospel of Christ.

CHAPTER XIV.

FUNG-SHUI.

Description of the Superstition.

No one can be long in China without hearing something of that gigantic and wonderful system of superstition known as Fung-shui, which, perhaps, more than anything else, dominates the Chinese people, holding many of them in a state of miserable bondage. You everywhere meet with evidences of its existence and influence ; but, however carefully you inquire, you fail to get any very intelligible definition or description of it. You try and ascertain the reason for some peculiar arrangement in building, the demolition of some recently erected structure, or the continuance of some great accumulation of refuse, which is a disfigurement and nuisance to a large district, and you are told that the reason has something to do with Fung-shui ; but if you push your inquiries, and ask what this Fung-shui is, almost every person you ask will give you a different answer. The dark thread of this superstition is woven warp and woof into the very fabric of Chinese life. It reveals its existence everywhere, and it seems to blend in various and mysterious ways with everything.

Archdeacon Moule, in his *New China and Old*

gives a description of this remarkable superstition. 'The word (Fung-shui) means literally "wind and water," and some say that it is so called "because it is a thing like wind, which you cannot comprehend ; and like water, which you cannot grasp "—a description true enough of the system, for its ramifications are indeed hard to comprehend. But the explanation is vague and improbable.

'The formulated system of Fung-shui has four divisions: *Li,* or the general *order* of Nature ; *Su,* her *numerical* proportions ; *K'i,* her vital breath and subtle energies ; *Hing,* her form, or outward aspect. The harmonious blending of these four would seem to contribute a perfect Fung-shui ; the contrary will produce calamity.   Three principles are laid down by the professors of this art, in which truth and error, religion and superstition, strangely mingle. (1) That heaven rules the earth. (2) That both heaven and earth influence all living beings ; and that it is in man's power to turn their influence to the best account for his own advantage. (3) That the fortunes of the living depend also on the good will and influence of the dead.   In direct connection with this third point comes in the superstitious part of ancestral worship.   Under *Li,* or order in Nature, the Chinese believe in the Reign of Law, and make much of the number five.   There are five elements ; five planets (Jupiter, Mars, Saturn, Venus, Mercury) ; five viscera ; five colours ; five kinds of happiness; and five relationships, namely, that between prince and minister, father and son, husband and wife, elder brothers and younger, and friend with friend.   As to

Su, the numerical proportions of Nature in ancient and modern Fung-shui literature are at variance. At the time of the *Yih-King*, the most ancient of the Chinese classics, they recognized, instead of five, six elements. The modern system of Fung-shui, formulated by Choohe (the great commentator on Confucius), and by others during the Sung dynasty (A.D. 1126–1278), endeavoured to harmonize the two ; and taking 10, or twice 5, as the sacred number for heaven, and 12, or twice 6 (or 8 + 4, the number of the two sets of mystic diagrams known to the ancients), as the sacred number for earth, they constituted ten heavenly stems, and twelve terrestrial branches, and from their combination composed the cycle of sixty names, which is used now to designate successive years. A clever geomancer, well versed in this intricate but meaningless array of formulæ, imposes with ease on his ignorant and superstitious customers.'

Archdeacon Moule refers to the curious fact that the profession and practice of this great and popular system of Fung-shui is denounced in the *Sacred Edict* as a capital crime.

This superstition is closely linked with the graves of China ; and as these are found everywhere, it is almost impossible to interfere with the existing order of things without exposing oneself to the very serious charge of disturbing the Fung-shui of the district. It is the universal belief that the spirits of the dead maintain very close and real relations to the living ; and if they find themselves involved in any discomfort, because a favourable site for their graves has not been chosen, or because these graves have been subsequently disturbed and interfered with, they will punish their descendants for their neglect by bringing upon them misfortunes of various kinds. If, then, the comfort and prosperity of a family are to be maintained, and if the spirits of wrathful and discontented ancestors are not to come back to worry and injure the surviving members of their families, great care must be exercised in choosing for them a burial-place, and in seeing that the burial-place is not interfered with after it has been well and wisely chosen. That no mistake may be made where the consequences of a mistake are so serious, the services of a Fung-shui man are requisitioned, who, upon receiving certain payments, will, according to the rules of the mysterious art which he professes, fix, perhaps after long delay, upon a site which, satisfying the dead, will bring good fortune to the living. Many things have to be taken into account, but especially the aspect of the site chosen. As good influences are supposed to come from the south, and evil influences from the north, the most favourable situation is a hillside facing the south.

Without going further into detail, it will be seen how this superstition stands in the way of modern improvement, the introduction of railways and telegraphs. When it was first proposed to establish telegraphic communication, strong and strenuous resistance was offered, on the ground that they would disturb the Fung-shui of the districts through which the telegraph wires were to be carried. But when, for military purposes, they were deemed needful, the telegraph posts and wires were set up, in the face of all superstitious objections. A line of telegraphic communication was carried through Shansi just before we visited that province, and we were told that very strong objections were raised. The Government, however, managed the business very well. Notice was given that the telegraph was to be introduced, that foreigners would be sent to erect it, and that each district was to provide posts and labour. With much grumbling, posts and labour were furnished, and the work was completed, and allowed to remain, the shrewd Chinese knowing well enough that if they were to destroy the work, they would have to supply posts and labour again. It was, however, commonly reported and believed that the foreigners had secretly buried a human head at the foot of each telegraph post, thus imparting to the wires the mysterious power they possess of conveying messages.

It will be easily seen how the influence of this superstition declares itself in almost every direction, and how suspicions are awakened by foreigners, who are credited with great powers, which they may exercise with very injurious effect, by interfering intentionally or ignorantly with the Fung-shui of the district in which they reside. There is nothing too marvellous for a Chinaman to believe; and nearly every Chinaman is the victim, to an extent that is to us almost incredible, of superstitious and childish fears. And so the erection or the removal of a wall may mean much more to the Chinese than to us; the erection of a wall in one place may mean the shutting off of good influences; the demolition of a wall in another place may mean the opening of a way for the invasion of evil and malign influences.

You constantly see a small cross wall built a little distance from the doorway of a house, either inside or outside, or both—serving as a screen—the intention of which is to safeguard the family against the ingress of evil spirits or influences, which, as they always move straight forwards, and never turn a corner, are effectually shut out by these interposed obstacles. The objection so strongly urged by the Chinese against the erection of lofty buildings by foreigners, rests on the ground that they will interfere with the Fung-shui.

The Fung-shui explains what occurs to us as a very strange custom common in some parts of China. Trouble comes upon a Chinese family, and it is declared by those who profess to know that the misfortune has resulted from the bad Fung-shui of the ancestral burial-ground ; and so the bones of the dead are taken up and deposited in earthen jars, in which they are kept, sometimes for years, till a new and more suitable burial-place has been selected.

Belief in this curious superstition of the Fung-shui is, we were assured, universal. We were constantly meeting with proofs of its widespread influence ; and large numbers of Fung-shui men, astute professors of this mysterious art, practise upon the credulity of their countrymen, with much profit to themselves, but to the serious loss and impoverishment of their victims. It is only as men enter into the liberty of the Gospel that they are liberated from the bondage of these superstitious fears.

CHAPTER XV.

MISSIONARY WORK AND METHODS IN CHINA.

MISSION work in China, so far as we had the opportunity of observing it, branches out into the three great divisions of evangelistic, educational, and medical work ; and, if we may speak of that separately, women's work among women, which, too, is evangelistic, educational, and medical. I would, however, like to say here, to prevent the possibility of misapprehension, that while, for convenience, evangelistic is distinguished from educational and medical work, that we saw no educational or medical work in China which was not emphatically and un-mistakably evangelistic in its character and aim, and, even so far as the gathering in of converts is concerned, satisfactory in its results. Some missions lay special stress on preaching, others on education, others on medical work, but I think it may be said that there is no mission in which all these branches of Christian work are not in varying proportions combined ; and the very distinct impression pro-duced upon our minds was that there is room and need for all, and that no branch of work can be omitted or neglected without serious loss and detriment to that great enterprise upon the success of which our hearts are supremely set.

EVANGELISTIC WORK.

Every mission feels that its work is to evangelize China ; but with oneness of aim and intention there is diversity of method. Where missions are located in large or considerable centres of population, there is the use, almost, I think, without exception, of the *street-chapel*, in which frequent, often daily, services are held. These services are somewhat free and easy in their character, the Chinese coming in and going out at their pleasure. We were present at many of these services, and were greatly interested in what we saw. The testimony of many of the oldest missionaries in China, American and English, with whom we conversed, was very distinct as to the value of these services. The knowledge of the gospel is thus often carried, by those who come in as casual hearers, far beyond the limits of the city where it is preached ; and missionaries in the interior frequently meet with those who have some knowledge of the ' doctrine '— who, when asked where they first heard of it, will refer to a street-chapel or book-shop in a city, distant, perhaps, hundreds of *li* from the place of their abode. After what we saw, and especially after what we heard from such men as Drs. Blodget, Corbett, Griffith John, Chalmers, and the Revs. Arnold Foster, W. Muirhead, and many others, we felt strongly that, whatever other methods of evangelization might be adopted, preaching in the street-chapel should not be neglected.

In addition to the street-chapel or preaching-hall, to which outsiders are invited, there is, usually, the Domestic Chapel, as it is called, devoted to the use of Christians and professed inquirers, and in which the more regular religious services are conducted.

Another way of reaching the Chinese in large towns and cities is by the *book-shop*. This is a shop, which should be situated in a good position in an important business street, where books and tracts, and sometimes small articles of stationery, are sold. In China you are at perfect liberty to enter a shop, and look round, and spend some time in it, though you have no intention of purchasing anything. And many well-to-do and educated Chinese, who would never think of entering a street-chapel, will readily enter a book-shop, and gratify their curiosity by looking at the books and tracts, the maps and pictures, that are exposed for sale, and will freely enter into conversation with the person or persons in charge, who have thus the opportunity of preaching the gospel across the counter.

But besides the shop, and screened off from it, there is, or should be, another room, comfortably furnished as a guest-room, into which the more interested inquirers can be invited, and there, with the inevitable cup of tea, and the almost as inevitable pipe of tobacco, such inquirers will sit for the hour together, receiving further instruction concerning the things of the kingdom. Where well conducted, the book-shop is a most valuable agency. Large numbers of Chinese are reached in this way who would probably be reached in no other, and while the results of such agency cannot be easily traced or tabulated, we may reasonably hope that much of the seed thus quietly and unobtrusively sown will, in different parts of this great empire, spring up and bear fruit.

We must be careful not to put any limited interpretation on the word 'preach,' when we insist on the importance of preaching the Gospel. According to nearly universal testimony, a great deal of the most valuable work is done in a very informal and incidental way—presenting the truth to little groups of people or individuals, met with on the wayside and elsewhere, just as Jesus preached the Gospel to the woman at the well, and Philip to the eunuch on the desert-road to Gaza. Travel is slow in China ; the necessity for stopping on the road is a frequently recurring one, and in an ordinary journey on the road, in the courtyards of inns, and the streets of villages and towns, which on market-days are always thronged, the missionary has many opportunities, of which he is not slow to avail himself, of preaching the Gospel ; and the word thus familiarly spoken is ordinarily associated with Bible and tract distribution.

An experienced missionary says with reference to work of this kind, ' It is encouraging on subsequent visits to hear repeated assurances that such or such a person has a book containing the doctrines preached. The reverence which the Chinese have for the printed character often leads them to accept the truth of a statement simply because it is made in a publication. The books thus distributed among the people form the subject of frequent conversation, and thus the name at least of our Saviour becomes familiar to many. This in itself is no small gain. It always makes one feel more certain that the message will be understood, where many Christian books have preceded the preacher, than in places where even the names and titles of the Saviour have to be explained.'

In addition to the work which is done (as it were incidentally) in those lengthened journeys which missionaries are from time to time compelled to take, there are carefully arranged and regularly recurring itinerating tours; and many missionaries spend a large portion of their time and energy in this itinerating work—work which in many parts of China has been crowned with very distinguished success.

A great deal of the evangelistic work is carried on by the natives themselves; and in the future *native agency* must be employed to an ever-increasing extent. Every one feels that, if China is to be evangelized, it must be by the Chinese themselves. The work can never be overtaken by foreigners. The great aim of the foreign missionary is, or should be, to make the work as largely as possible, and as speedily as possible, self-supporting and self-propagating; to awaken and strengthen in the minds of the natives a sense of responsibility; and to make them feel that, in receiving the gospel for themselves, they have been put in trust with it for others. That

missions can be made to a large extent self-supporting and self-propagating, the records of the Amoy
and Shantung Missions abundantly prove. We had
the opportunity of looking carefully into the work
of the English Baptist Mission in Shantung, which
is to a larger extent than any other mission we
saw self-supporting and self-propagating. Both in
the Tsing-Chow-fu district and the Chow-ping district the work is done chiefly by the natives themselves ; and so many and so widespread are the
native communities under their care, that our foreign
missionaries can do little more than exercise an
episcopal influence and superintendence. In the
Tsing-Chow-fu district there are seventy-nine centres,
where Christians and inquirers meet. There are
1200 Church members and many inquirers, un-
equally distributed over a district as large as York-
shire. In Chow-ping, where the work is much more
recent, there are, in a district of about the same
size, ninety-nine centres, some 1100 enrolled inquirers, and several hundred Church members. All
the work within the Church area is done by the
natives themselves, and entirely at their own cost.
About a dozen evangelists are paid by the society
for work done outside that area, and they are paid
such small sums that the most suspicious of their
fellow-countrymen would not entertain the idea
that they engage in the work for the sake of the
remuneration they receive.

The question as to the employment of a paid
native agency is a difficult one, and one as to which
opinion is somewhat divided. That the millions of

China can only be brought to Christ by Chinamen every one admits ; and also that it is the duty of foreign missionaries to develop native agency to the fullest possible extent, and to make the most of it in every direction. But they must do this in such a way as to impress upon the mind and conscience of the native Church the fact that the work of propagating the Gospel must depend very largely upon the spontaneous efforts of private Christians, who by life and word shall bear testimony for Christ in their different walks of life. The universal testimony of missionaries in the field is that, for the present at least, there must be to some extent the employment of a paid native agency ; and there is nearly as complete a consensus of opinion that the greatest discretion should be used in employing it. Some, however, feel much more strongly than others as to the propriety, and even the necessity, of rigidly limiting expenditure in that direction. Dr. Griffith John, with his large experience, says, 'Keep the staff of paid agents as low as possible. And the rule of the Shantung Baptist Mission seems a wise one—to limit the expenditure of foreign money to work done beyond the Church area. Let all other paid native workers learn that they must live on Chinese, and not foreign money.'

EDUCATIONAL WORK.

All the missionary societies in China are engaged in doing educational work to a larger or less extent —some spending a large amount of effort and money upon it, making it a very conspicuous part of their

Q

work; while some other societies, not entirely neglecting it, bestow upon it a disproportionately small measure of attention. Missionaries in China, as elsewhere, have this work forced upon them. If there is to be a strong, self-supporting, self-propagating Church established in China, the work of education cannot be neglected. There must be a fairly well-educated class trained up, from which the leaders and teachers and pastors of the Church shall ultimately be taken.

When, since my return, I have spoken about the importance of educational work in China, I have been met again and again with the inquiry as to whether there was any very urgent need for it. Are not the Chinese a well-educated people? it has been asked. This idea is a very prevalent one. In the *Multum in parvo* Atlas for 1890 I read, 'In China Proper few are unable to read and write.' This is a great mistake. In a paper read by the Rev. J. C. Gibson before the Shanghai Conference this question is carefully dealt with ; and, according to him, if by reading we are to understand the intelligent perusal of a simply written and non-technical book, not more than ten per cent. of the men of China can read, and not more than one per cent. of the women. This is considered a very liberal estimate. Dr. Martin, of Peking, gives a much lower one—five per cent. of men, and one in 10,000 of women. In mixing with native congregations we were struck by the considerable number who seemed to be able to use Hymn-book and Bible; but we were assured that the great majority of these had learned to read after they became Christians.

In the Baptist Mission we have not gone very largely into educational work. What is done divides itself into three branches—village day-schools with native teachers, one-half of whose small salary is provided by the parents of the children ; a boarding-school, in which a more advanced education is given to selected children of native Christians, whose parents pay one-third of the cost of their board— five out of fifteen dollars, the amount which would about keep them at home. We have also a small training-college to fit teachers, evangelists, and pastors for their work, to the support of which institution the native Church has liberally con-tributed out of its extreme poverty. In our Mission instruction is only given in the Chinese language. This saves the pupil from the temptation to use a knowledge of English as a mere marketable com-modity, and obliges him to live among his people and exert his influence upon them. Another advan-tage is that a strictly Chinese education, given in a school where all live in Chinese fashion, has little tendency to lift its possessor above the level of the people with whom he will have to live, and those extremely simple and frugal modes of life to which he will have to conform himself. There is room for all kinds of work in China ; but, from all we heard and saw, we were led to feel strongly that missionaries would be wise to limit themselves to education in the Chinese language, and to avoid everything which shall have even a tendency to make the pupils discontented with the unadorned simplicity and plain and frugal fare of the homes in which they have been brought up, and of those in which of necessity they must hereafter dwell.

MEDICAL WORK.

This, again, is a very important branch of mission work in China, and, like educational work, while it receives much more attention from some societies than others, it is, so far as we know, entirely neglected by none. Having been for many years somewhat closely associated with hospital work in England, I naturally availed myself of every opportunity that presented itself of inquiring into and inspecting hospital and dispensary work in China ; and I am glad to be able to bear testimony to the great value of that work, not only as a medical and benevolent, but also, and still more as an evangelizing, agency. Before going to China, I shared in some degree the fears entertained by many, that the medical missionary, in the enthusiastic prosecution of his medical work, is in danger of forgetting that he is a missionary as well as a medical man, and that after a while, though working as an agent of a missionary society, he will be little more than a medical man, doing good, useful, much-needed work, but not missionary or evangelistic work. But now, having met and conversed with many medical missionaries, having lived in their homes, having spent many hours with them in their hospital, dispensary, and evangelistic work, I feel how utterly groundless that fear was. Some of the most devout, devoted, enthusiastic men we met were medical missionaries— men in whom scientific and medical enthusiasm was

not quenched, but men whose souls were aflame with
love for Christ, and love for the perishing around
them for whom Christ died. We did not meet with
a single man in connection with any society who
did not evidently feel that he was first of all a missionary. To use the words of one of the finest men
we met with, 'the medical missionary is not merely
a doctor—he is an evangelist; and if faithful to
Christ, he will be blessed to the salvation of souls.'

No one who has not been to China can form any
idea of the extent and urgency of China's need in
this particular, and how largely this special form of
Christian benevolence has been appreciated by the
Chinese people. But we value the work not only
because of the enormous amount of suffering it has
been the means of alleviating, but also and especially
because it is one of the most useful of the evangelizing
agencies employed. Large numbers, who would not
and could not have been reached in any other way,
have been brought under Christian instruction, and
within the range of Christian influence, through the
instrumentality of the medical missionary. The
work thus done breaks down prejudice, weakens
opposition, inspires confidence, and makes a way for
the Gospel into many a Chinese home and many a
Chinese heart, into which otherwise it would not
have gained an entrance. And if we limit our
attention to direct spiritual results—cases of conversion which issue in baptism and Church membership
—medical missions will compare very favourably
with any other branch of mission work.

In speaking of medical missions, I ought not to

be silent as to the valuable service rendered by our medical missionaries, and missionaries with some measure of medical knowledge, in dealing with the great opium curse. It is impossible to say what proportion of the people are addicted to this vice. In the province of Shansi, one of the great opium-producing provinces, the habit is fearfully common. I only refer to this subject now, that I may remind my readers that in all the hospitals of China large numbers of opium-patients are treated; and, in addition to hospital work, there have been established in different parts of the empire many opium-refuges, into which those who are anxious to be set free from the bondage of this vile habit are received. In our intercourse with foreigners we met occasionally with those who attempted to justify the trade in opium, insisting that the effects of its use were not so bad as some represented them to be ; but, on the other hand, we were impressed by this remarkable fact, that while in the course of our travels we spoke with many who used opium, we never met a Chinaman who had a word to say in defence of the practice. As to the feeling of the Chinese themselves in reference to this habit, I would quote a sentence or two from a paper by Dr. Dudgeon, a great authority. He says, ' The Chinese government and people, smokers and non-smokers alike, regard it as a vice, a curse, and their greatest plague. Not one word is ever spoken in defence of it. It is universally condemned in the most unqualified manner. The very devotees of the drug feel ashamed that they are addicted to the slavery. The Chinese of no class regard opium as so many foreigners do. At the ports, or after a short trip in the interior, foreigners speak with the assurance of those who " know all about it." I have never met with a Chinese who approved of it or advocated it. All sorts of excuses are heard from foreign apologists —they tell us it is a valuable solace to the poor, sweetening, soothing, and ameliorating their condition, and in many cases curing disease. China's experience and observation of a century universally condemns it. Opium-smokers are among the most miserable people that visit our hospitals. The Chinese testimony is much stronger than any condemnation by us of the drinking habits of the West.' We have reason to be thankful that, while as a nation we must take shame to ourselves because of the part played by our Government in forcing opium upon China, our missionaries are doing all they can to check the progress of an evil which is a greater curse in China than drunkenness is in England.

I have only one word more to say about hospital and dispensary work in China—and that is the almost incredibly small cost at which it is carried on. From a number of Reports lying by me, I give two or three examples.

Peking Hospital, London Missionary Society, 1888–89, treated 10,561 out-patients, and three hundred and nineteen in-patients, inclusive of opium-smokers, at a cost of 503.13 taels, as shown in balance-sheet ; but to this should be added a further charge of three hundred taels for English medical stores, which should have been included in that year's account.

St. Luke's Hospital, Shanghai, American Episcopal.

The report of 1889 shows that 20,279 out-patients were treated, and five hundred and eleven in-patients, including one hundred and thirty surgical cases, and this at a cost of rather less than $2000.

C. I. M. Hospital, Chefoo. One hundred and twenty in-patients, chiefly surgical, and 6000 out-patients, at a cost of $550.

And it should be remembered not only that these institutions are worked in an extremely simple and economical manner, but that a very large proportion, in some instances the entire amount, of even this small cost is met by local subscriptions, foreign and Chinese. Altogether there was scarcely any department of missionary work which impressed us more favourably than that carried on by the medical missionaries in the hospitals and dispensaries we had the privilege of visiting.

WOMEN'S WORK AMONG WOMEN.

An increasing measure of attention is being directed to this important branch of work by all the missionary societies in China. We came away from China profoundly impressed with the splendid opening there is for women's work, the urgency of the need for it, and the fact that there is a great deal of work that can only be done by devoted and duly qualified women who shall be specially set apart for the doing of it. There is a very prevalent idea in this country that the need for women's work in China is not nearly so great and urgent as in India; whether that be so or not I cannot say, for I have never been in India, but I can say that the need of China in this respect is very great and very urgent. Well-to-do women are scarcely ever seen outside their own doors ; the women of the labouring class are commonly seen attending to the different duties of life in the neighbourhood of their own homes, working and gossiping in the streets, walking on the roads, working in the fields. But with the feeling prevalent in China as to the separation of the sexes, the women of the upper classes may be said to be absolutely inaccessible by male missionaries, and women of the lower classes, even, difficult to approach. Women must be reached by women, either by the wives of missionaries, or by women who specially devote themselves to the work. While, then, it cannot be said that women in China are completely beyond the reach of the male missionary, it may be said that, *as a rule*, women can only be reached and successfully dealt with by women ; and most would feel and be ready to admit that if China is to be largely and permanently influenced by the Gospel, the women must be reached.

And China is open to women. At this moment splendid work is being done by women. At the time of the Shanghai Conference, May, 1890, there were seven hundred and seven women at work in China, three hundred and ninety-one wives of missionaries, three hundred and sixteen single women ; and that number has since been considerably increased. The work of women in China, like that of men, branches out as evangelical, educational, and medical, and in each department women are rendering inestimable service.

Do you ask how women carry on their evangelistic work? I would say that a women with her heart full of love for Christ, and of tender, yearning compassion for her suffering sisters, will by persistent inquiry discover, or with holy ingenuity invent, numberless ways of preaching and commending the Gospel; and with womanly tact will carry on her work in such a modest and unobtrusive way as to offend as little as possible the Chinese sense of propriety. Do you ask how an English or American woman gets into and finds a welcome within a Chinese home? You can no more describe her mode of entrance than you could that of the morning sunlight, or the sweet and genial breath of spring. You only know that she does get in, and that the whole house is the sweeter, brighter, better, for her presence.

Women are doing in China a good and much-needed *educational work*, and we were glad to hear that it is a work which is being more and more fully appreciated by the Chinese. Miss Noyes, of Canton, in a paper on Girls' Schools, read at the Shanghai Conference, quotes the words of an educated Chinese gentleman who had graduated with honour in a Western land, and who had seen and appreciated what Christianity and education can do for women. He says, 'The question of female education in China is of especial interest to me. I believe the crying need of China is the elevation of her women, and their liberation from the social shackles that bind them. She must remain stagnant so long as she allows her daughters to be made household drudges, and denied the right and opportunity to cultivate and cherish an interest in things beyond the four walls of their homes. That those who need help most should be helped first, is a truth as old as the hills, and as trite and undeniable as that two and two make four. My countrywomen should have the first claim on the attention, sympathy, and charity of Christian people in more favoured lands. That they have not had the consideration they deserved in the schemes for the evangelization of China, is inexplicable to me. The seed of a man's faith in the providence of God is planted in his heart by his mother, and no one else can do it half as well. And it is needless to say that the surest way of bringing China into line with America and Europe is by giving to her daughters the advantage of a Christian education.' The need, the claim, of the girls of China could not be better put. The work has been commenced—may it go on and prosper! We had many opportunities of inspecting girls' day and boarding schools carried on by different missionary societies, and we were delighted by what we saw.

One of the most important and successful branches of women's work in China is the *medical* work, for which there is great room and great need. For while, yielding to the urgency of painful and long-continued disease, Chinese women will consult and submit to the treatment of a foreign and male physician, there can be no doubt that they do so very reluctantly, and would much prefer to be treated by doctors of their own sex. And medical work among the women, perhaps even more than among the men, is a most important evangelistic agency. In hospital and dispensary work there is a fine opportunity for preaching the Gospel, presented not only to the lady-physician and her helpers, but also to the Chinese Bible women who are usually associated with them, of which they gladly avail themselves.

But besides hospital and dispensary work, fully qualified medical ladies, and even those who are only partially qualified, find that their medical knowledge secures for them entrance to and influence within many Chinese homes that otherwise would be absolutely closed against them. It is a great help to any woman working in China to have even a limited knowledge of medicine. Many remarkable instances were brought under our notice which went far to show that the women of the wealthier and more influential classes can scarcely be reached in any other way.

I have been able to touch only upon a few salient points, and to convey very imperfectly a few of the strongest impressions produced upon my mind by this brief visit to China, and the glimpses we got of mission work in that wonderful empire. And I would just say, in conclusion, that I was especially impressed by three things : the greatness of the opportunity set before the Christian Church ; the urgency of China's spiritual need ; and the satisfactory and encouraging character of the missionary work which we were permitted to see.

No words can adequately set forth the greatness of the opportunity with which the Christian Church is confronted. The present is a great crisis of opportunity. China is open to the presence and labours of Christian men and women, and to the touch of Christian influence, as she has never been before. And the question which presses upon us as Christian people is this : whether, with this splendid opening for service, and this loud and imperative call to service, we are ready to go in and possess the land ?

No one can visit China, live in China, even for so short a time as we did, without feeling not only what a magnificent opportunity is presented to us, but also the greatness and urgency of China's spiritual need. There are many who question the existence of such a need ; there are some who deny it. They say to us, ' Have not the Chinese a splendid system of morality ? Are not the Chinese people, according to your own admission, a law-abiding, contented, industrious people, with some good features of character which Western people might with some advantage imitate ? And their superstitions, if foolish, are they not comparatively innocent and harmless ? They have got on fairly well without you for 4000 years ; why push yourselves in where your presence is not wished for or needed ? ' A visit to China would, I think, convince any one not wilfully blind that she needs the Gospel fully as much as any nation under heaven, and that the Gospel is able to give to China and do for China what nothing else can. The Chinaman is practically, if not professedly, a secularist, an agnostic, with certain superstitious and idolatrous additions, which are accepted and observed out of a prudential regard for self or a politic consideration of others ; and with this prevailing agnosticism, the

moral conscience of the people is not so much perverted as paralyzed. One who knows China well
has said, ' What the Chinese lack is not intellectual
ability. It is not patience, practicability, or cheer-
fulness, for in all these qualities they greatly excel.
What they do lack is character and conscience.'
And I need scarcely say that nothing else than the
Gospel, nothing less than the Gospel, will meet
China's need.

And now there is the further question, How far
is the Gospel, as sent to China, and as preached in
China by the different missionary societies, meeting
that need? How far are Christian missions touching
the life of the nation, effecting any real change, conferring any real benefit? In a word, how far are
they able to justify their existence by pointing to
tangible, visible, appreciable results? I have sought
to answer that question in what I have written.
And I can only say again what I have said before,
that what we saw, for extent, character, and worth,
far exceeded our largest expectations, and, so far from
feeling that we had been deluded by exaggerated
and garbled statements, we felt, as we passed from
one mission station to another, that the half had not
been told us.

A strong appeal is being made by all missionary
societies for large and speedy reinforcements. In
the presence of the great opportunity which is presenting itself, it will be a grievous pity if through
lack of funds the men and women needed for the
service of Christ in this great empire are not sent
out. It will be a still more grievous pity if all the

men and women needed for this service are not forth-coming at the call of duty and of Christ. We cannot believe that we have exhausted the resources of the Church, or that we have reached the limit of Christian willinghood. May we not hope that, on the necessities of the case becoming more widely known, there will be no lack of men or women or money ?

China needs the Gospel. The door of this great empire, long closed against us, has, in God's provi-dence, been thrown wide open, and the question which is pressing upon us and waiting for our reply is, Are we ready to go in and take possession of the land in Christ's name ? There are difficulties, there are hindrances many and great, many things doubtless will occur to try both faith and patience ; but there is opportunity for service, there is the unmistakable call to service, and He who calls us to engage in His service has given us the promise of all needed assistance in it, and the assurance of victory and reward. When we think only of China's millions, and the difficulties which seem to rise mountainous and insurmountable in our way, we are ready despondingly to exclaim, 'Who is sufficient for these things ? ' But when we remember that it is in the Lord's name and in the Lord's strength that we engage in this great enterprise, we can say, 'Who art thou, O great mountain? Before a Church divinely inspired and divinely sustained thou shalt become a plain ; ' and 'He shall bring forth the headstone thereof with shoutings of Grace, grace unto it,' *for* 'It is not by might, nor by power, but by My Spirit, saith the Lord of hosts.'

APPENDIX.

SUMMARY OF PROTESTANT MISSION WORK IN CHINA, FROM REPORT OF THE SHANGHAI CONFERENCE, MAY, 1890.

FOREIGN MISSIONARIES.

Men	589
Wives	391
Single Women . .	316
Total . .	1,296

NATIVE HELPERS.

Ordained . . .	211
Unordained . . .	1,266
Female Helpers . .	180
Total . .	1,657

MEDICAL WORK.

Hospitals . . .	61
Dispensaries . .	44
Native Students . .	100
Patients in 1889 .	348,439

CHURCHES.

Organized Churches . .	522
Self-supporting—	
Fully . . .	94
One-half . . .	22
One-third . . .	27
Total . . .	665

BIBLE DISTRIBUTION.

Bibles . . .	1,454
New Testaments .	22,402
Portions . . .	642,000
Total . .	665,856

Tract Distribution .	1,287,227
Religious Journals .	12
Pupils in Schools .	16,836
Communicants .	37,287
Contributions by Native Christians in 1889	$36,884.54

GROWTH OF MISSION WORK IN CHINA.

(Dr. Morrison went to China in 1807.)

In 1842 there were . . .	6	Communicants.
,, 1853 ,, . . .	350	,,
,, 1865 ,, . . .	2,000	,,
,, 1876 ,, . . .	13,035	,,
,, 1886 ,, . . .	28,000	,,
,, 1889 ,, . . .	37,287	,,

LONDON : PRINTED BY WILLIAM CLOWES AND SONS, LIMITED,
STAMFORD STREET AND CHARING CROSS.

For EU product safety concerns, contact us at Calle de José Abascal, 56–1°,
28003 Madrid, Spain or eugpsr@cambridge.org.

www.ingramcontent.com/pod-product-compliance
Ingram Content Group UK Ltd.
Pitfield, Milton Keynes, MK11 3LW, UK
UKHW010341140625
459647UK00010B/755